Literacy Objectives

3

Madeleine Birch
Melinda Derry
Michael Duffy
Harry Webb

Melinda Derry (Series Editor)
David McLaughlin (Series Consultant)

Longman

Pearson Education
Edinburgh Gate
Harlow
Essex
CM20 2JE

England and Associated Companies throughout the World

ISBN 0 582 52988 3

First published 2003

Printed in Great Britain by Scotprint
Haddington

The publisher's policy is to use paper manufactured from sustainable forests.

Cover: Getty Images/Art Wolfe

Sources and acknowledgements

Texts

We are grateful to the following for permission to reproduce copyright material:

Amazon.com Inc for a review of *Harry Potter and the Philospher's Stone* by Karin Snelson published on www.amazon.com; British Heart Foundation for extracts from "HACK!" leaflet © BHF; Channel 4 Television for extracts from "don't panic" and "just ask" published on www.channel4.com; DK Images for the spread on mountain building from *Eyewitness Science: The Earth* by Susanna Van Rose; Emap and Nintendo Official Magazine for an extract from "Star Wars Rogue Leader: Rogue Squadron II" HMV's Gamecube Launch Special leaflet; Faber and Faber and Farrar, Straus & Giroux Ltd for the poems "Six Young Men" by Ted Hughes from *Selected Poems 1957-1981* by Ted Hughes and "MCMXIV" by Philip Larkin from *Collected Poems* by Philip Larkin; Good News Family Care for an extract from www.gnfc.org.uk; Guardian News Service Limited for the articles "TV violence on the increase" by Jason Deans published in *The Guardian* 29th January 2001 © Guardian, "First have an identity" by John O'Farrell published in *The Guardian* 6th October 2001 © John O'Farrell, "Your health…lets raise a glass to it" published in *The Observer* 17th February 2002 © Observer, "What does it mean to me? Nothing, nothing, nothing" by Leone Ross published in *The Guardian* 19th July 2002 © Leone Ross and "Pleasethankyouwotnopardon" by Binyavanga Wainaina published in *The Guardian* 19th July 2002 © ; Independent Newspapers (UK) Limited for the article "There is no need to panic about identity cards" by Kaizer Nyatsumba published in *The Independent* 4th July 2002; Nature for an extract from "Blow for teens' TV time" by John Whitfield published on www.nature.com 29th March 2002 © Macmillan Publishers Ltd; Oxfam Publishing 274 Banbury Road, Oxford OX2 7DZ UK for the leaflets "Make a gift for life" and "Four hours spent in an Oxfam shop will pay for enough vaccinations to immunise twelve children against six diseases"; Penguin Books Limited for extracts from *Happy Days with the Naked Chef* by Jamie Oliver; The Random House Group Limited for an extract from *Touching the Void* by Joe Simpson published by Jonathan Cape; Scholastic Children's Books for extracts and pictures from *Horrible Geography: Freaky Peaks* by Anita Ganeri © Anita Ganeri 2001, illustrated by Mike Phillips © Mike Phillips 2001 and Trinity Mirror for the article "It's the two Ronnies" by Martin Lipton published in the *Daily Mirror* 1st July 2002;

Photographs

David Wootton Photography: pp.7, 8, 10, 12, 14, 16; Hulton|Archive/Getty Images: pp.18, 20, 22, 24, 26; Getty Images/Art Wolfe: pp. 39, 40 (far left), 42, 44, 46, 48, 50, Getty Images/SW Productions: p.113, Getty Images/Sion Touhig: pp.133, 134 (far left), 136, 138, 140, 142, Getty Images/Scott Barbour p.135 (bottom right); Moviestore/Lucas Films: pp.122, 124 (far left), 126, 128, 130, 132; Rex/Mansell: p.40 (top left); Clive Streeter: p.40 (bottom left); robertharding.com: p.40 (bottom right); Konrad Wothe/OSF: p.41 (middle right); David Loftus: pp.51, 52, 54, 55, 56, 58, 60; Tim De Waele/Corbis TempSport: pp.61, 62 (far left), 64, 66, 68, 70, 71, 72; Jon Gardey/ Robert Harding/Alamy: pp.75, 76 (far left), 78 (far left), 80, 82, 84, 86; Validate UK: p.88 (top right); PA Photos/Toby Melville: p.88 (middle); BBC Photograph Library: pp.111, 112, 114, 116, 118, 120; Bloomsbury/Thomas Taylor (cover illustration): p.123; Sola Coard: p.134 (top middle); The Caine Prize for African Writing: p.135 (top).

Picture Research by Danielle Pulver

Illustrations

Sam Hadley (Artist Partners) p.27 and p.87, Peter Greenwood (Advocate) p.97.

Contents

Imagine, explore, entertain

As you prepare for your key stage 3 tests and look beyond to your GCSEs you will find that, increasingly, you are being asked to encourage a particular response in your reader. Writing to imagine, explore and entertain is writing in which the writer seeks to engage, amuse and interest the reader by appealing to his or her imagination and sense of enquiry.

Writing to **imagine** often invites its readers to visualise situations, people and places which may well be outside their personal experience. Writers who produce imaginative writing will employ a varied range of language and literary devices in a way that enables their readers to put themselves successfully in an unfamiliar situation, thereby sharing the experience.

When you are writing to **explore**, often you will be responding to something that you have read yourself and exploring your own reactions to it. Many GCSE English Literature questions will ask you to explore your ideas about the texts which you have studied, as indeed will the Shakespeare reading question in your key stage 3 test. In the sense that you may be examining ways in which you think a writer may have seen or imagined a particular situation, writing to explore is closely related to writing to imagine.

Most writers would hope to **entertain** their readers, even when the primary purpose of the writing might be to communicate information or instruct a reader how to do something. Writing which is not entertaining often remains unread! Almost any kind of writing is more likely to be successful if it tries to engage and entertain its reader. Entertaining writing often attempts to involve a reader by adopting a particular attitude or tone, which encourages a response.

In the next three units, you will notice how these different types of writing share many common features and that techniques used in one type of writing might be equally effective when used in the others.

Unit 1: Imagine

It is unlikely that many of us will ever have been in the situation of Simon and Joe in the extract from Joe Simpson's book, *Touching the Void*, which you are going to read in this unit. The extract features a climbing accident, which leaves one of the mountaineers, Joe, dangling from a cliff face and the other, Simon, desperately trying to rescue him. The writer helps the reader to **imagine** the feelings going through the minds of the two characters by telling the story from both men's perspectives, thus helping us to share their experiences and imagine what our own reactions to the situation might be. Before you read, think about a time when you have been in a frightening situation. With a partner, discuss the words which describe the emotions you felt.

Simon's account

Joe Simpson, an experienced mountaineer, has injured his leg whilst climbing. Here, his companion, Simon, is lowering him down on a rope. Everything is going well until Joe falls, almost pulling Simon out of his seat cut into the snow.

Suddenly I jolted heavily forward from the waist and nearly came out of the seat. I threw my weight back and down into the snow, bracing my legs hard against the sudden pressure. Joe's fallen. I let the rope slide slowly to a stop, trying to avoid the impact I would have got if I had stopped it dead. The pressure remained constant. My harness bit into my hips, and the rope pulling tautly between my legs threatened to rip me down through the floor of the seat.

After half an hour I let the rope slide again. Whatever Joe had gone over had stopped him getting his weight off the rope. My legs had numbed as the pressure on my hips cut the blood supply away. I tried to think of something to do other than lower. There was nothing. Joe had not attempted to climb back up. I had felt no trembling in the rope to tell me he was attempting something. There was no chance of hauling him up. Already the seat was half its original size. It had steadily disintegrated from beneath my thighs. I couldn't hold the weight much longer. The steep sections higher on the face had been less than fifty feet high. I decided that he would be able to get his weight off the rope after a short distance, and set a belay up. I had no choice.

As the rope ran out I realised that the pressure wasn't easing. Joe was still hanging free. What in hell's name was I lowering him over?

I looked down at the slack rope being fed through the belay plate. Twenty feet below I spotted the knot coming steadily towards me. I began swearing, trying to urge Joe to touch down on to something solid. At ten feet I stopped lowering. The pressure on the rope hadn't changed.

I kept stamping my feet. I was trying to halt the collapse of the seat but it wasn't working. I felt the first shivers of fear. Snow hit me again from behind, surging over and around me. My thighs moved down fractionally. The avalanche pushed me forward and filled the seat behind my back. I'm coming off.

Then it stopped as abruptly as it had started. I let the rope slide five feet, thinking furiously. Could I hold the rope with one hand below the knot and change the plate over? I lifted one hand from the rope and stared at it. I couldn't squeeze it in to a fist. I thought of holding the rope locked against the plate by winding it round my thigh and then releasing the plate from my harness. Stupid idea! I couldn't hold Joe's weight with my hands alone. If I released the plate, 150 feet of free rope would run unstoppable through my hands, and then it would rip me clear off the mountain.

It had been nearly an hour since Joe had gone over the drop. I was shaking with cold. My grip on the rope kept easing despite my efforts.

The rope slowly edged down and the knot pressed against my right fist. I can't hold it, can't stop it. The thought overwhelmed me. The snow slides and wind and cold were forgotten. I was being pulled off. The seat moved beneath me, and snow slipped away past my feet. I slipped a few inches. Stamping my feet deep in to the slope halted the movement. I had to do something!

The knife! The thought came out of nowhere. Of course, the knife. Be quick, come on, get it.

The knife was in my sack. It took an age to let go a hand and slip the strap off my shoulder, and then repeat it with the other hand. I braced the rope across my thigh and held on to the plate with my right hand as hard as I could. Fumbling at the catches on the rucksack, I could feel the snow slowly giving way beneath me. Panic threatened to swamp me. I felt in the sack, searching desperately for the knife. My hand closed round something smooth and I pulled it out. The red plastic handle slipped in my mitt and I nearly dropped it. I put it in my lap before tugging my mitt off with my teeth. I had already made the decision. There was no other option left to me. The metal blade stuck to my lips when I opened it with my teeth.

I reached down to the rope and then stopped. The slack rope! Clear the loose rope twisted round my foot! If it tangled it would rip me down with it. I carefully cleared it to one side, and checked that it all lay in the seat away from the belay plate. I reached down again, and this time I touched the blade to the rope.

It needed no pressure. The taut rope exploded at the touch of the blade, and I flew backwards into the seat as the pulling strain vanished. I was shaking.

Leaning back against the snow, I listened to a furious hammering in my temple as I tried to calm my breathing. Snow hissed over me in a torrent. I ignored it as it poured over my face and chest, spurting into the open zip at my neck, and on down below. It kept coming. Washing across me and down after the cut rope, and after Joe.

I was alive, and for the moment that was all I could think about. Where Joe was, or whether he was alive, didn't concern me in the long silence after the cutting. His weight had gone from me. There was only the wind and the avalanches left to me.

When at last I sat up, the slack rope fell from my hips. One frayed end protruded from the belay plate – he had gone. Had I killed him? – I didn't answer the thought, though some urging in the back of my mind told me that I had. I felt numb. Freezing cold, and shocked into a numb silence, I stared bleakly into the swirling snow beneath me wondering at what had happened.

Dictionary check

belay a wedge or pin used to secure rope to

belay plate a special plate in the shape of a figure 8 used to wind rope on to

knot a large intertwined piece of rope which wouldn't fit through the belay plate

Joe's account

I lolled on the rope, scarcely able to hold my head up. An awful weariness washed through me, and with it a fervent hope that this endless hanging would soon be over. There was no need for the torture. I wanted with all my heart for it to finish.

The rope jolted down a few inches. How long will you be, Simon? I thought. How long before you join me? It would be soon. I could feel the rope tremble again; wire-tight, it told me the truth as well as any phone call. So! It ends here. Pity! I hope somebody finds us, and knows we climbed the West Face. I don't want to disappear without trace. They'd never know we did it.

The wind swung me in a gentle circle. I looked at the crevasse beneath me, waiting for me. It was big. Twenty feet wide at least. I guessed that I was hanging fifty feet above it. It stretched along the base of the ice cliff. Below me it was covered with a roof of snow, but to the right it opened out and a dark space yawned there. Bottomless, I thought idly. No. They're never bottomless. I wonder how deep I will go? To the bottom ... to the water at the bottom? I hope not!

Another jerk. Above me the rope sawed through the cliff edge dislodging chunks of crusty ice. I stared at it stretching into the darkness above. Cold had long since won its battle. There was no feeling in my arms and legs. Everything slowed and softened. Thoughts became idle questions, never answered. I accepted that I was to die. There was no alternative. It caused me no dreadful fear. I was numb with cold and felt no pain; so senselessly cold that I craved sleep and cared nothing for the consequences. It would be a dreamless sleep. Reality had become a nightmare, and sleep beckoned insistently; a black hole calling me, pain-free, lost in time, like death.

My torch beam died. The cold had killed the batteries. I saw stars in a dark gap above me. Stars, or lights in my head.

The storm was over. The stars were good to see. I was glad to see them again. Old friends come back. They seemed far away; further than I'd ever seen them before. And bright; you'd think them gemstones hanging there, floating in the air above. Some moved, little winking moves, on and off, on and off, floating the brightest sparks of light down to me.

Then, what I had waited for pounced on me. The stars went out, and I fell. Like something come alive, the rope lashed violently against my face and I fell silently, endlessly into nothingness, as if dreaming of falling. I fell fast, faster than thought, and my stomach protested at the swooping speed of it. I swept down, and from far above I saw myself falling and felt nothing. No thoughts, and all fears gone away. So this is it!

A whoomphing impact on my back broke the dream, and the snow engulfed me. I felt cold wetness on my cheeks. I wasn't stopping, and for an instant blinding moment I was frightened. Now, the crevasse! Ahhh ... NO!!

The acceleration took me again, mercifully fast, too fast for the scream which died above me ...

The whitest flashes burst in my eyes as a terrible impact whipped me into stillness. The flashes continued, bursting electric flashes in my eyes as I heard, but never felt, the air rush from my body. Snow followed down on to me, and I registered its soft blows from far away, hearing it scrape over me in a distant disembodied way. Something in my head seemed to pulse and fade, and the flashes came less frequently. The shock had stunned me so that for an immeasurable time I lay numb, hardly conscious of what had happened. As in dreams, time had slowed, and I seemed motionless in the air, unsupported, without mass. I lay still, with open mouth, open eyes staring into blackness, thinking they were closed, and noting every sensation, all the pulsing messages in my body, and did nothing.

I couldn't breathe. I retched. Nothing. Pressure pain in my chest. Retching, and gagging, trying hard for the air. Nothing. I felt a familiar dull roaring sound of shingles on a beach, and relaxed. I shut my eyes, and gave in to grey fading shadows. My chest spasmed, then heaved out, and the roaring in my head suddenly cleared as cold air flowed in.

I was alive.

From *Touching the Void* by Joe Simpson

Dictionary check

crevasse a deep, open crack in thick ice
disembodied free from the body

T Text level: reading

Looking from different perspectives

> By telling the story from both men's perspectives, the writer is using the technique of **multiple narration.** This technique allows the reader to follow the experiences and emotions of more than one character. It also enables the reader to look at the same events through the eyes of different characters.

1 In Simon's account, Simon describes the various problems he encounters, and how he responds to them; whilst in Joe's account, Joe describes the effects Simon's actions have on him. Copy and complete the following table by listing all the problems Simon faces, his responses to them and the effect they have on Joe. The first one is done for you.

Simon's problem	His response	Effects on Joe
Joe falls, almost pulling Simon out of his seat.	*Simon throws his weight back and braces his legs hard.*	*Joe is held dangling on the rope below Simon.*

2 What are Simon and Joe's emotions before the rope is cut? Choose one word to describe each man's feelings and give reasons for your choice.

3 Read closely the section of Simon's account which deals with the cutting of the rope from 'The knife!' to 'I was shaking.' on page 9. Pick out three quotations from this section and explain how they help to create a sense of fear and tension.

4 Explain how Joe shows what happens after the rope is cut. You should comment on:
 • the way the physical sensations he experiences are described
 • the way he describes his thoughts and how these change
 • the way he shows the speed at which events happen.

5 The two men's different perspectives are perhaps most vividly shown in the endings of each account. Which do you feel is the more effective in involving the reader? Give reasons for your opinions.

 Word level

Using verbs to make an impact

Sometimes writers can use verbs to create different effects and give information. Some verb forms tell you the time of the action and who carried out the action.

> **Example**
>
> *Leaning back against the snow, **I listened** to a furious hammering in my temple as **I tried** to calm my breathing.*

The verb form used here shows who is performing the verb (Simon) and when it happened (in the past). These are examples of the **finite form of the verb**.

Other verb forms don't give you this information.

> **Example**
>
> ***Leaning** back*

The forms of the verb which don't tell you when the action is happening are called **non-finite verbs.**

The verb 'leaning' could be used to describe an action in the past ('was leaning'), present ('is leaning') or future ('will be leaning'). Here it is the **auxiliary verb** ('was', 'is' and 'will be') that shows the tense.

1 Identify the non-finite verbs used in the following sentences and comment on their effect.

   a) Fumbling at the catches on the rucksack, I could feel the snow giving way beneath me.

   b) Snow hit me again from behind, surging over and around me.

   c) I let the rope slide, thinking furiously.

2 Rewrite the following sentences by changing the finite verbs into non-finite verbs. The first one is done for you.

   a) I lolled on the rope, scarcely able to hold my head up.
   Lolling on the rope, I was scarcely able to hold my head up.

   b) I stared into the abyss and saw only flurries of snow in the blackness.

   c) Snow enveloped me like a blanket and it encased me in a pocket of pure whiteness.

3 Briefly explain what effect changing the finite verbs to non-finite forms has on each of the sentences in question 2.

S Sentence level

Paragraph organisation

Writers frequently organise and develop their paragraphs in such a way that different sentence structures, when placed together, may create different effects. Look again at the following paragraph from Joe's account:

Example

Another jerk. Above me the rope sawed through the cliff edge, dislodging chunks of crusty ice. I stared at it stretching into the darkness above. Cold had long since won its battle. There was no feeling in my arms and legs. Everything slowed and softened. Thoughts became idle questions, never answered. I accepted that I was to die. There was no alternative. It caused me no dreadful fear. I was numb with cold and felt no pain, so senselessly cold that I craved sleep and cared nothing for the consequences. It would be a dreamless sleep. Reality had become a nightmare, and sleep beckoned insistently, a black hole calling me, pain-free, lost in time, like death.

The writer uses a succession of short, simple sentences at the beginning of the paragraph to create a sense of thoughts crowding into Joe's mind.

This is followed by two more complex sentences, suggesting more considered reflection, or more detailed analysis of the situation.

The use of the semi-colon throws emphasis back on to the subject of the main clause. The numbing effects of the cold in the first sentence, and the seductiveness of sleep in the second sentence.

1 Look again at the paragraph in Joe's account which begins 'Then what I had waited for pounced on me …'. Explain how the organisation of sentences in this paragraph helps to create a dramatic effect.

You should comment on:

- sentence lengths and types
- where in the paragraph different types and lengths of sentences are placed
- the use of punctuation within the longer sentences.

2 Now look at the paragraph beginning 'It had been nearly an hour since Joe had gone over the drop …' in Simon's account. Explain how the organisation of sentences in this paragraph differs from the paragraph in Joe's account beginning 'Another jerk.'

You should comment on:

- the way the two paragraphs open
- the types and lengths of sentences used
- the order in which the sentences appear and what effect this has
- the way the paragraphs end
- which paragraph would have a greater impact on a reader.

3 Rewrite the paragraph from Joe's account beginning 'Another jerk.' Use longer, more complex sentences at the beginning of the paragraph and shorter, simple sentences at the end. Explain how you think the changes you have made would affect the way a reader might respond.

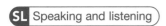 Speaking and listening

Conducting a successful interview

Joe and Simon have been rescued and are going to be interviewed about their experiences. You are going to work in a group of three. One of you will play Joe, one Simon and the other the TV interviewer.

In your group devise a series of questions to ask both Joe and Simon, which will enable them to develop an account of their own feelings at various stages of the incident described in the extracts. Try to focus upon their different perspectives of the same events.

- Think about ways in which you might link your questions. For example, a question which invites Simon to explore his feelings about the seriousness of the situation when he realised that Joe had fallen might be followed by one to Joe, which encourages him to talk about what his feelings were immediately after falling.

- The interviewer could ask Joe and Simon to speculate at different stages how they thought the other might be feeling. You might decide to sequence the questions chronologically.

When you have agreed on two sets of questions to ask Joe and Simon, act out the role-play of the TV interview. When you have completed your interview, discuss how successful the questions were in gaining the answers you expected.

Writing to imagine

 Writing: minor task

> In your key stage 3 tests you will have to answer questions that ask you to comment on the writer's use of language. Write a two-paragraph answer to the following question about the two extracts you have read.

Comment on how successful each account is in allowing the reader to experience the drama and tensions of Simon's and Joe's experiences.

You should comment on:

- the use of different sentence types in the two accounts
- the way paragraphs are organised
- the effects of the language used in each account.

> Remember to refer back to the work you did on the use of different sentence types and paragraph organisation in the Sentence level section on pages 14–15. Also think about the work you completed in the Word level section on the impact of non-finite verbs on page 13.

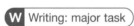 Writing: major task

The two accounts you have read in this unit give you different narrative perspectives of the same event. When the extracts finish, Simon is sitting near the cliff face, having just cut Joe loose, staring 'bleakly into the swirling snow beneath … wondering what had happened.' Joe has fallen to the bottom of the cliff but although in pain is still alive.

You are going to continue the story and show what happened to Simon and Joe. You should use the technique of multiple narration and write some paragraphs from Simon's point of view and the other paragraphs from Joe's point of view.

The writing frame on the next page will show you how to do this.

What you could include

- Start by adopting Simon's narrative viewpoint.
- Explore the thoughts and feelings going through Simon's mind from the end of the extract.
- What might be some of his fears about what has happened to Joe?

- The next paragraph should adopt Joe's narrative viewpoint.
- Show Joe's amazement at his survival.
- Describe his physical condition and his impressions of his surroundings.
- Consider how Joe's perspective will differ from Simon's.

- Think about what Simon would do next. Would he try to reach safety? Go for help?
- What will his feelings be about Joe at this stage?

- Return to Joe's perspective.
- How will he react to his predicament? Will he attempt to move or remain where he is and hope for rescue?

- Bring the story to a logical and appropriate conclusion. Perhaps each narrator might be rescued or reach safety.
- Maybe Joe and Simon could be reunited at the end or perhaps you can imagine a more dramatic or unusual ending.

How you could write it

- **Contrast descriptions of Simon's physical sensations with descriptions of his feelings.**
- **Choose effective vocabulary to create a sense of Simon's fear and tension.**
- **You could use short rhetorical questions to show the different thoughts crowding Simon's mind.**

- **Again you might use vocabulary to describe Joe's relief at his survival but also to communicate his fears.**
- **You could use short sentences to show Joe's confusion, mixed with more complex sentence structures to show analysis of the situation.**

- **Try to construct and organise your paragraphs to show the build-up to Simon's decision.**

- **You could use short rhetorical questions to show how Joe considers his different options.**

- **Maintain the technique of alternating narrative viewpoints all the way through the story.**
- **At times you might be able to show the characters' different perspectives on the same event.**

Unit 2: Explore

We often find photographs particularly powerful in evoking a sense of time and place; they can recall strongly a great many feelings and emotions. In both of the poems which you will read in this unit, the writers **explore** the feelings which a photograph creates for them. In the first poem, 'MCMXIV', the poet, Philip Larkin, describes the scene of young men being recruited into the army at the start of the First World War. In the second poem, 'Six Young Men', Ted Hughes describes an old photograph showing a group of friends taken before they went off to fight in the First World War. In these poems the writers go beyond the visual impact of the photographs to explore a more personal view of the different thoughts that the pictures have stimulated for them about the First World War.

Pre-reading

Look carefully at the photograph on the opposite page. Working with a partner, discuss what feelings the photograph evokes for you.

- What sort of relationship is there between the people in the photograph?
- How can you tell that it is an old photograph?
- What do you think the people are feeling?
- What do you think happened to them?

MCMXIV

Those long uneven lines
Standing as patiently
As if they were stretched outside
The Oval or Villa Park,
The crowns of hats, the sun
On moustached archaic faces
Grinning as if it were all
An August Bank Holiday lark;

And the shut shops, the bleached
Established names on the sunblinds,
The farthings and sovereigns,
And dark-clothed children at play
Called after kings and queens,
The tin advertisements
For cocoa and twist, and the pubs
Wide open all day –

And the countryside not caring:
The place names all hazed over
With flowering grasses, and fields
Shadowing Domesday lines
Under wheat's restless silence;
The differently-dressed servants
With tiny rooms in huge houses,
The dust behind limousines;

Never such innocence,
Never before or since,
As changed itself to past
Without a word – the men
Leaving the gardens tidy,
The thousands of marriages,
Lasting a little while longer:
Never such innocence again.

Philip Larkin

> **Dictionary check**
>
> **Domesday** a survey of all the land in England carried out in the eleventh century

Six Young Men

The celluloid of a photograph holds them well –
Six young men, familiar to their friends.
Four decades that have faded and ochre-tinged
This photograph have not wrinkled the faces or the hands.
Though their cocked hats are not now fashionable,
Their shoes shine. One imparts an intimate smile,
One chews a grass, one lowers his eyes, bashful,
One is ridiculous with cocky pride –
Six months after this picture they all were dead.

All are trimmed for a Sunday jaunt. I know
That bilberried bank, that thick tree, that black wall,
Which are there yet and not changed. From where these sit
You hear the water of seven streams fall
To the roarer in the bottom, and through all
The leafy valley a rumouring of air go.
Pictured here, their expressions listen yet,
And still that valley has not changed in sound
Though their faces are four decades under the ground.

This one was shot in an attack and lay
Calling in the wire, then this one, his best friend,
Went out to bring him in and was shot too;
And this one, the very moment he was warned
From potting at tin-cans in no-man's land,
Fell back dead with his rifle-sights shot away,
The rest, nobody knows what they came to,
But come to the worst they must have done, and held it
Closer than their hope; all were killed.

Here, see a man's photograph,
The locket of a smile, turned overnight
Into the hospital of his mangled last
Agony and hours; see bundled in it
His mightier-than-man dead bulk and weight:
And on this one place which keeps him alive
(In his Sunday best) see fall war's worst
Thinkable flash and rending, onto his smile
Forty years rotting into soil.

That man's not more alive whom you confront
And shake by the hand, see hale, hear speak loud,
Than any of these six celluloid smiles are,
Nor prehistoric or fabulous beast more dead;
No thought so vivid as their smoking blood:
To regard this photograph might well dement,
Such contradictory permanent horrors here
Smile from the single exposure and shoulder out
One's own body from its instant and heat.

Ted Hughes

Dictionary check

ochre-tinged yellowing stains
trimmed ready
hale healthy

Comparing viewpoints

1 Read through both poems. Write a paragraph giving your initial impressions about the subject matter of each poem. What do you like or dislike about each poem?

2 **a)** Both poems use a photograph as a means of visualising a bygone era. Copy and complete the following table by picking out the details from the poems that help you to picture the period in which they are set.

MCMXIV	Six Young Men
moustached archaic faces	*their cocked hats are not now fashionable*

b) Pick two details from each poem and briefly explain how they help to create a picture of the period for you.

3 Re-read the opening stanza of 'MCMXIV'.

a) What do you think are the 'long, uneven lines' which Larkin mentions in the opening line? Look back at the photograph on page 18 to help you.

b) What two comparisons does Larkin make when he uses the words 'as if'? What do these comparisons suggest about the mood of the people?

4 In the first three stanzas of 'MCMXIV', Larkin builds up a picture of life in Britain in 1914, before the First World War.

a) Pick out three details that suggest the innocence of life then.

Example

... August Bank Holiday lark

b) How do these three stanzas help you to understand the fourth and final stanza?

c) Discuss the fourth stanza with your partner. Why do you think Larkin ends the poem with the line 'Never such innocence again.'?

5 Re-read the opening two stanzas of 'Six Young Men'.

    a) What does the photograph in the Hughes poem show?

    b) What similarities are there between the photograph in this poem and the images in the opening stanza of 'MCMXIV'?

6 Look closely at the third stanza of 'Six Young Men.' Write down what happened to each of the men in the poem.

7 Read closely the final two stanzas of 'Six Young Men'. In this part of the poem, Hughes contrasts the everyday images from the photograph ('the locket of a smile') with the horror of what happened to the men ('hospital of his mangled last agony').

    a) Pick out the other contrasting images from the final two stanzas.

    b) Choose one pair of contrasting images and briefly explain what they make you feel.

    c) What do you think Hughes means when he writes 'To regard this photograph might well dement'? What does this show about his feelings?

8 Think about your answer to the first question in this section. Have your initial ideas about the poems changed? Write a paragraph summarising what you now think about the subject matter of each poem.

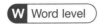 Word level

Creating tone and mood

The **tone** of a piece of writing is the attitude that the writer has towards his or her subject matter. Writers convey tone through their choice of words, lengths of sentences, sentence complexity, and other elements. When writers write in the **third person**, using careful observation and description and avoiding emotive vocabulary, this is called writing in an **impersonal tone**.

> Example
>
> *And the shut shops, the bleached* ← Written in the third person
> *Established names on the sunblinds,*
> *The farthings and sovereigns,* ← Exact description with no explicit comment on it
> *And dark-clothed children at play*
> *Called after kings and queens ...*

An impersonal tone can create a sense of distance between the writer and the reader and this is effectively employed by Larkin to create the **mood** of a past time.

1 Look at the first two stanzas of the poem 'Six Young Men'.

   a) What sort of tone does Hughes use in the first stanza of the poem? Select quotations to support your answer.

   b) Does the tone change in the second stanza? If so, how does the writer achieve this?

   c) What mood do you think Hughes is trying to create in the first two stanzas?

2 As the poem 'Six Young Men' progresses, Hughes employs a more personal and emotional tone.

   a) Pick out quotations that suggest a more personal and emotional tone is being used.

   b) What words would you use to describe Hughes' attitude to the subject matter of his poem? You could choose from the words given below or use your own.
   • sad   • angry
   • amazed   • horrified

S Sentence level

Using quotations effectively

One of the important skills required for success in your key stage 3 tests is the ability to respond to texts, analysing writers' techniques, commenting on features of language and structure and their effect on the reader. You need to support your arguments and opinions by providing evidence quoted from the text to develop and explain your points. The sequence of an effective analytical sentence is as follows:

- first of all make your **point**

- then provide an **example** which illustrates it from the text

- then develop your point by **explaining** how the example illustrates the point.

Look at the following sentence which analyses the first stanza of Ted Hughes' poem 'Six Young Men':

Example

Even though the photograph itself has become 'faded and ochre-tinged', time will not have 'wrinkled the faces or the hands' of the young men, who are effectively captured in a frozen moment in time and will never age.

Opens with the point that the photograph may grow old.

Illustrates opening point with a quotation from the poem.

Develops the point with the explanation that the men in the photograph will always look as they did when it was taken, integrating a further brief quotation.

1 Write brief paragraphs using short quotations to answer the following questions about the poem 'MCMXIV':

a) How does Larkin create a feeling of normality in the opening stanza?

b) How does Larkin give his reader a sense of regret in the final stanza?

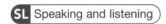

Comparing ideas and sharing information

You are going to work in a group of three. In your group you are going to discuss either Philip Larkin and his poem 'MCMXIV' or Ted Hughes and his poem 'Six Young Men' and answer the following question:

What is the poet's view of the effects of the First World War?

In your discussion you should consider how the poet you have chosen to discuss felt about the effects of the First World War on:

- individuals
- society in general
- future generations.

You should choose one member of your group to act as a scribe to note down the main points. When you have finished your discussion, organise the notes into a clear and logical order. Then join with another group which has been discussing the other poet and present your findings to them. Finally, as a group of six, discuss the main similarities and differences between each poet's views on the effects of the First World War, making notes as points are raised.

Writing to explore

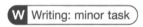

Look back at the notes you made for the Speaking and listening activity. You are now going to write three paragraphs which compare and contrast Hughes' and Larkin's attitudes to the effects of the First World War:

In your paragraphs you should:

- focus on the final stanza of each poem for your material
- comment on the different tone each poet adopts
- comment on the different ways in which each poet uses language to affect his reader's feelings
- use quotations to support your points and develop your ideas.

W | Writing: major task

Imagine that you are one of the people in the photograph – you might be a friend of one of the soldiers or a relative. Twenty years on the photograph is all you have left to help you remember that day.

You are now going to write a piece of prose in two sections, one written about how you felt at the time of the photograph, and one about how you feel twenty years later. In this piece of prose you should explore how you would respond if you had seen your friend or relative join the army and then go on to be killed in action. You will then write a short poem about the person who was killed. This could be included in an obituary about the person or on their gravestone.

What you could include

First section: Then

- Start by describing what the photograph shows.
- Describe the way you felt on that day, watching your friend or relative join the army.
- Explain how the photograph captures their personality.

Second section: Twenty years later

- Explore how you feel looking at the photograph now, twenty years later.
- Describe how the place where the photograph was taken has or hasn't changed.
- Describe how your friend or relative died.

Third section: Poem

- Try to sum up what you feel about the person you have lost.
- Try to convey to people who didn't know the person what they were like.

How you could write it

- Write in the third person, as if you were looking at the photograph. Use similes and metaphors.
- Change to the first person to explain how you felt at that time.
- Use the present tense to describe what is happening in the photograph as if it was happening now.

- Use phrases such as 'It is twenty years since ...'.
- Use sentences linked together by connectives which describe the contrast of then and now.
- Use short sentences to convey the action of the event, including effective adverbs and adjectives.

- Focus on an image that sums up the person's qualities.
- You could include suitable phrases from your piece of prose.

Unit 3: Entertain

Often writers have more than one purpose for their writing. For example, we tend to think of non-fiction texts as giving us serious information about something or instructing us how to do something. It is very common, however, for writers to present non-fiction in a way which is both visually **entertaining** and uses language that adds humour for the reader, so that the information is more likely to be understood.

The two texts you are going to read present information about health matters in different entertaining ways. The first is taken from a leaflet which seeks to present the dangers of smoking to its readers. The second is taken from *The Observer* newspaper and comments on the way in which information about the dangers to our health seems to change. Before you read, discuss with a partner the health hazards you are aware of.

A–Z of smoking leaflet

RISK

Take 10 young people who start smoking in their teens and carry on throughout their lives. What are they likely to die of?

- It is very unlikely indeed that any of them will be **MURDERED**
- And none will die in a **RADIATION LEAK** from a nuclear power station
- None will be killed by a **TERRORIST BOMB**
- And none will die in a **WAR**
- Almost certainly none will die in a **CAR CRASH** or from **AIDS**
- **But 5 of the 10 will die before their time from diseases caused by SMOKING CIGARETTES.**

| War | Source: based on estimates by Prof. Richard Peto |

SMOKE FREE AIRWAYS

A large majority of passengers want smoke free flights.

So major airlines such as British Airways, Sabena and Swissair are now completely smoke free.

Smoking is banned on all flights within the US.

| June 9 – Don't Smoke In Cars Day | Source: GLOBALink |

TAIWAN

A company in Taiwan has patented a coughing ashtray, designed to put people off smoking.

Every time a smoker flicks ash into the tray, it starts a major coughing fit.

Can **YOU** think of an invention that would put people off smoking?

| Heart | Source: *New Scientist* |

UNDERAGE SMOKERS

The Government takes more than £100 million a year in taxes from young smokers.

This is about the same as tobacco companies spend in the UK on adverts and promotion. For them, it's an excellent long-term investment. The younger a person starts smoking, the more likely it is that they will carry on paying out for cigarettes throughout their life.

| Video | Source: *British Medical Journal* |

# VIDEO

Whenever someone lights up a cigarette on screen, it may not be because the storyline needs it. It's more likely that the tobacco industry paid the film makers big money for it to happen.

This is a very powerful method of advertising. Named cigarette brands feature in many Hollywood films.

In fact, films get seen more on video than at the cinema, which makes them even better for tobacco companies – the videos get shown all round the world, and they get round any advertising bans or age restrictions at the cinema.

Videos get shown in the home, over and over again, often to very young children. This way the tobacco industry reaches far more people than go to the cinema.

| Image | Source: Health Education Authority |

WAR

Cigarettes love war. British soldiers first took up smoking in a big way during the Crimean War (1853-56).

They picked up the habit from Turkish gunners, who rolled tobacco in paper and used them to light the gunpowder in their cannon. Between firings, they sucked on the cigarette to keep it alight.

During the First World War (1914-18), and again in World War Two (1939-1945), troops were given a ration of cigarettes. War ended, but smoking didn't.

Now nearly twice as many Britons die every year from cigarettes than died per year in World War

eX-smokers	Source: *Tobacco in History*, J. Goodman

eX-SMOKERS

The number of people who smoke is far smaller now than 50 years ago.

In 1948, about 2 in every 3 **men** smoked cigarettes. That was their peak year. For **women**, the peak year was 1966, when over 4 in every 10 women smoked. Since then numbers have gone down – **mostly because loads of people have given up. There are now more eX-smokers than smokers.**

SMOKING: A DYING HABIT

% of over-16s in Great Britain who are regular cigare

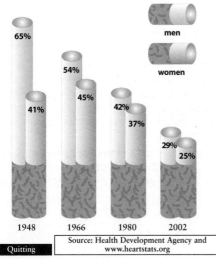

men

women

65% 41% (1948)
54% 45% (1966)
42% 37% (1980)
29% 25% (2002)

Quitting	Source: Health Development Agency and www.heartstats.org

Y-FRONTS

Every year about 1500 children in Britain are found to have cancer.

It is likely that about 150 of these cancers would not have happened if their fathers hadn't smoked. Men who smoke produce fewer sperm – on average, about 24% fewer. And it's not just quantity. Sperm (and the DNA they contain) arc more likely to be damaged. Researchers have found that about 1 in 10 of childhood cancers (including leukaemia) could be due to the cigarettes smoked by fathers-to-be.

The more the dads smoke, the bigger the risk to their children.

Atmosphere	Source: University of Birmingham

ZZZZZZ

People who live with smokers are more likely to miss out on their beauty sleep – smokers are six times more likely to snore.

Image	Source: *Cigarettes: What The Warning Label Doesn't Tell You*, ASCH

If you would like more information about how to take good care of your heart, write to the British Heart Foundation, 14 Fitzhardinge Street, London W1H 6DH

HACK! was created for the British Heart Foundation by Comic Company www.comiccompany.co.uk Words: Philip Boys. Design: Corinne Pearlman. Illustrations: Woodrow Phoenix, Graham Higgins. The author and artists assert their right to be identified as creators of the work.

M12/2A 5/2002

Your health ...
... let's raise a glass to it

What a week it has been for those of us who thought our lifestyles were a blueprint for longevity. Every day, new tales of unlikely health advice. Fruit and veg cause cancer! Apples rot your teeth! Sun good for you! Sleep kills! Our post-festive regime – yours, too, we feel sure – relied heavily on steamed broccoli, eschewing chocolate in favour of a crisp Granny Smith, bed by 10 o'clock every night and (not difficult at the moment, we admit) protecting bare skin from harmful UV rays. All wrong. All foolishly counter-productive.

As we report today, those prescribed five fruit and veg were a Trojan horse for nitrates likely to cause gullet cancer. We could have staved it off if only we'd allowed ourselves to absorb a little vitamin D from the Sun. The apple that kept the doctor away was rotting our tooth enamel and enriching our dentists. If we'd stuck with the chocolate, it would have lowered our blood pressure and spring-cleaned our arteries. Early nights? Every hour over eight was lopping years off our lives. Years, don't forget, in which we could have gourmandised, sunbathed and partied all night. Pass that antioxidant St Estèphe.

From *The Observer*

Dictionary check

blueprint for longevity formula for a long life
post-festive regime routine after Christmas
eschewing giving up
counter-productive having the opposite of the desired effect
prescribed recommended

nitrates a type of fertilizer
gullet throat
staved fought
gourmandised eaten a lot for pleasure
antioxidant a substance that prevents oxygen causing tissue damage
St Estèphe a French wine

T Text level: reading

Working out purpose and audience

1 What messages about health are given in each of the texts? Write two sentences summarising the content of each text.

2 Look again at the headline of *The Observer* column. How does this link to the content of the column?

3 Re-read the first paragraph of the column. Why do you think the writer has chosen to include a series of exclamatory sentences? Explain what effect you think they will have on the reader.

4 What do you think the purpose of this column is and who is the audience at which it is aimed? You should comment on:

- the headline
- what the column is about
- the vocabulary used.

5 Look again at the section of the A–Z leaflet headed 'Y-FRONTS'.

a) Pick out some of the statistics that the writer includes here. What effect does including these statistics have on the reader?

b) How does the writer make the information seem shocking?

c) Explain why you think the designer of the leaflet has included the two cartoons in this section.

6 Thinking about your answers to question 5, briefly explain how this helps you to work out:

a) the audience the leaflet is aimed at

b) the purpose of the leaflet.

7 Which of the two texts do you find most effective at presenting information about health in an entertaining manner? Give reasons.

 W Word level

Implied meanings

Writers often use vocabulary to contribute to a personal and amusing tone. Sometimes they may **imply meanings** which are not explicitly stated. Look at the first sentence from *The Observer* column where the writer's choice of vocabulary implies his or her attitude towards the preoccupation some people have with healthy lifestyles.

Example

What a week it has been for those of us who thought our lifestyles were a blueprint for longevity.

The use of the **pronouns** 'us' and 'our' imply that the writer also shares this view.

Implies that a healthy-living regime is a carefully planned formula for long life.

1 Re-read the opening paragraph of *The Observer* article.

Copy and complete the following table by picking out the vocabulary that seems to imply the writer's attitude towards healthy living. For each example, explain what the attitude implied is and why you think this. The first one is done for you.

Vocabulary	Use in text	Attitude implied	Explanation
Tales	*New **tales** of unlikely health advice*	*The information is unreliable.*	*We usually use the word 'tales' to talk about fictional stories or untrue gossip.*

As well as using vocabulary which implies attitudes which are not explicitly stated, writers also use devices such as metaphors to suggest more specific meanings. At the beginning of the second paragraph the writer refers to a fruit and vegetable diet as a:

Example

Trojan horse for nitrates likely to cause gullet cancer

This refers to the legend of the ancient Greek soldiers, who hid in a large wooden horse to surprise and destroy the city of Troy. Here the writer implies that these nitrates are an unseen danger, concealed within an apparently harmless exterior. By using the metaphor of the Trojan horse the writer reveals that some things we had previously considered healthy, like a fruit and vegetable diet, can, in fact, be very bad for us.

2 Re-read *The Observer* column and then write sentences which contain metaphors to show the effects of:

a) sleep   **c)** chocolate

b) apples   **d)** sun.

3 In what other ways does the writer create a personal and amusing tone? Pick out examples from the text to support your answer.

Presenting information entertainingly

Leaflets often have to communicate a large amount of information in a limited amount of space in a way that the reader finds accessible. The casual reader can be put off by long stretches of unbroken writing so information in leaflets is often broken up into smaller chunks.

The *A–Z of Smoking* leaflet follows a logical pattern. Each section is clearly headed to alert the reader of its content, sometimes in an entertaining and humorous way which leads the reader in to the information given.

> Example
>
> *SMOKE FREE AIRWAYS*

This heading has a double meaning and could refer not only to airlines banning smoking, but also to our own 'airways'. This kind of play on words is called a **pun**.

1 Scan the leaflet to find another pun that is used. Explain what the effect of this pun is.

2 Write new headings for the following sections using amusing puns.

   a) Taiwan   **b)** Underage Smokers   **c)** Video.

3 **a)** The *A–Z of Smoking* leaflet presents information using several different presentational techniques. Copy and complete the following table by listing the different ways it presents information and explaining the impact of each technique.

Technique	Impact on reader
Use of headings	*Short, snappy phrases that stand out. Makes the reader want to read on to find out the connection between the heading and the information. Sometimes amusing, e.g. 'Y-FRONTS'.*

b) Number the presentational techniques you have identified into rank order (greatest impact = 1). Which do you think is the most effective presentational technique used and which is the least? Give reasons for your answer.

SL Speaking and listening

Preparing a speech

You are going to prepare a speech which looks at both sides of the question 'Should we spend less time worrying about our health and more time enjoying life?'

To plan your speech, use the information from both texts and any other research which you can carry out. When you have completed your planning, think about the techniques you can use to present the information in your speech in an interesting and engaging way for the audience. You should:

- structure your speech into separate sections, each dealing with one key point
- try to adopt the tone used in *The Observer* article to entertain and include your audience
- incorporate statistical evidence and expert opinions to support different sides of the argument
- end with a conclusion which considers all the evidence and gives your answer to the original question.

When you have practised the speech, present it to the rest of the class. When you have made your speech, think about how effective it was. A good way to analyse the effectiveness of a speech is to think about the comments and questions that are asked by the audience.

Writing to entertain

 Writing: minor task

Look again at the section of the *A–Z of Smoking* leaflet headed 'SMOKING: A DYING HABIT' which provides a graph illustrating how the incidence of smoking has declined over the last fifty years.

Using the information from this graph, write a brief explanation text entitled 'Smoking: A Dying Habit'. In this essay you should outline how smoking has declined and explain how the smoking habits of men and women have changed over time.

Write your essay in a formal tone, including the facts from the graph and suggestions about why the pattern of smoking has changed over time.

 Writing: major task

Your school has decided to mount a healthy-eating campaign and has offered a prize to the pupil who produces the most entertaining leaflet promoting healthy eating. The leaflets will be judged on the way they present information in a humorous and amusing way.

First you need to research the topic of healthy eating. Think about where you could find out reliable information that would be of interest to school pupils.

When you have completed your research, you will need to plan the layout of your leaflet. Look again at the *A–Z of Smoking* leaflet on pages 28–29. Think about the different presentational techniques used here and any others that you could use.

- How can you organise your leaflet into sections with appropriately entertaining headings?
- How much written text will you use and where should it be placed?
- Can you provide some information in graph or chart form?
- Will you include amusing cartoons or photographs to support the information?

Use the writing frame on page 36 to help you to plan your leaflet.

What you could include	How you could write it
• You could begin by giving examples of the effects of unhealthy eating. Remember to choose appropriate examples for your audience. • Include quotations from experts such as doctors and other health experts.	• **Try to include some medical vocabulary to add to the authority of the information you present, but remember to explain it for the reader.** • **You could include metaphors to communicate the information more effectively.**
• Give examples of healthy diets. • Explain what the benefits of healthy eating are. • Include statistics to support your examples.	• **Try to create a personal and entertaining tone by using personal pronouns such as 'you', 'we' and 'us'.** • **You could embolden the key information that you want to emphasise.**
• You could include case studies which show how healthy eating has helped individuals. • Include quotations from people who have changed the way they eat in order to follow a healthier diet.	• **Use adverbials of time, such as 'then' and 'now', to show how healthy eating gradually changed the individual's lifestyle.**
• Conclude with a reminder of why it is important to eat healthily. • Include a short, snappy slogan about healthy eating that people will remember.	• **Use words that imply the benefits of healthy eating.** • **Try to include a pun that gets your message across in an entertaining way.**

Help box

① Try to create an engaging and entertaining tone through your choice of vocabulary.

Review of revision objectives

Sn4 Integrate speech, reference and quotation

In your key stage 3 English tests you will need to be able to:

▶ carefully select precise words or phrases from the text to back up the point you are making, so that the quotation is short and to the point

▶ analyse the quotation to show how it links to the point you are making.

Look at this question about the texts in Unit 1. Then read Adam's answer.

Look again at the opening paragraph of each account. What differences are there between the way Joe describes what happens immediately after he falls and the way Simon describes it? Pick out words and phrases to support your answer.

> Joe describes how he felt after he fell. He says that, 'I lolled on the rope, scarcely able to hold my head up. An awful weariness washed through me and with it a fervent hope that this endless hanging would soon be over … I wanted with all my heart for it to finish'. <u>This shows that Joe wanted to die because he had been hanging there for too long.</u> Simon's account is different, because he does not describe what he felt but what he did. He describes what happened after Joe fell, 'Joe's fallen'. Then he says he, 'let the rope slide slowly to a stop trying to avoid the impact I would have got if I had stopped it dead. The pressure remained constant'. <u>Here he is saying that he was trying to protect Joe in case he was alive.</u>

1 a) Does Adam punctuate the quotations he uses accurately?
  b) Look at the first quotation that Adam uses. Could it be shortened?

2 Adam makes two important points:
  • that Joe describes his feelings, not his actions, after he fell
  • that Simon describes his actions, rather than how he felt.

  a) Do Adam's quotations back up the points he is making?
  b) Are all Adam's quotations necessary?
  c) Do Adam's explanations of the quotations he has selected (underlined) link back to the points he was trying to make?

3 To reach a level 5 you need to 'select quotations from the text and make references to them that are relevant to the point being made'. To reach level 6 you need to 'select short quotations which are used to support and develop specific points'. Award a level to Adam and explain why you think he is working at this level.

Inform, explain, describe

In this section you will be looking at writing that seeks to inform, explain and describe. The texts you will read in this section are very different – you will be studying information about how mountains are formed, looking at recipes and reading descriptions of a football match – so why are they grouped together?

The answer is that texts that are designed to **inform** the reader, such as the 'Mountain building' text from *Eyewitness Science: Earth,* often include sections of explanation and some detailed and lively descriptions to support the information given. Writers such as Jamie Oliver and his Victorian predecessor, Mrs Beaton, set out to **explain** how to cook, but along the way they add in lots of important information about food and some memorable descriptions of their dishes. Similarly, reports of events such as the World Cup final not only **describe** what happened, but they also explain why events happened in the way that they did.

Although the writers of these texts mix and match genres within them, they don't ignore the conventions of how to write each genre. Each of them pays close attention to how the text is organised. For example, if the text's main purpose is to describe, it won't focus on explanation because that's not what the reader is looking for.

Once you have mastered the technique of blending together these three genres to construct different types of text, you will be well on the way to becoming a skilful writer, able to turn your hand to a whole variety of writing for new purposes and audiences.

Unit 4: Inform

You are constantly being presented with writing that **informs** you and it often comes in very different contexts. It might be the information you find about the holiday destination you are planning to visit or it might be the information you find when exploring a website to help you with your homework. This unit explores how very similar information has to be presented in very different ways, depending on the audience for whom it is intended. You will read a serious, factual account of how mountains are created from the book *Eyewitness Science: Earth* and then look at the same information, this time from the book *Freaky Peaks*, which is written in a way that is likely to hold the interest and attention of younger readers. Before you read, think about the different techniques the writers of these texts might use to present the information.

Mountain building

GEOLOGISTS ONCE THOUGHT that the folded structures in mountain ranges showed that the Earth was shrinking, and they likened mountain ranges to wrinkles on a shrivelling apple. It is now known that mountain ranges are made up of rocks that have been stacked up and deformed into complicated structures, and that the Earth is not shrinking because new crust is being made in the oceans all the time (pp.38–39). Usually there is more than one generation of deformation in the making of a mountain range, so that folds become refolded. Broad common features of mountain ranges are that the foothill rocks are recognizably sedimentary (pp.26–27), while the middle of the ranges have more complicated rocks and structures – these rocks may be intensely deformed and recrystallized (pp.24–25). Young mountain ranges at active plate boundaries (pp.36–37) may have volcanoes sitting atop all the deformed structures. There is certainly a great deal of crushing and shortening of the crust in mountain building. However, deformation and uplift in themselves do not create the jagged peaks that are recognizably mountains. Erosion (pp.54–55) of many kilometres thickness of rock from the top of the rising land mass exposes the deep core of the mountain range. The entire process that makes mountain ranges is called orogenesis.

CROSSING THE ALPS
The Swiss physicist and explorer Horace Benedict de Sassure (1740-1799) crossed the Alps 17 times in different places to try to understand how mountain ranges are created. In the end, he decided that mountains were a hapless jumble and that to understand their structures was beyond possibility.

Upper parts of fold have been eroded

Sediment layers used to be horizontal

FOLD MOUNTAINS
Mountains show layers of sediments that have been folded into complex shapes. These vertical strata in southern England were folded at the same time as the Alps were formed a long way to the south.

THE ROCKY MOUNTAINS
In the late 19th century it was assumed that some of the crustal shortening of mountain ranges was brought about by one set of rocks being pushed over another set. This is called thrusting, and involves large-scale near-horizontal movements of the upper crustal layers. This seemed a far-fetched idea, but it turned out to be right. The structures in the Rocky Mountains involve multiple thrusting, one mass on another. It is hard to imagine how these great movements could be accomplished in material as hard and brittle as rock. The upper section of rocks that is pushed in thrusting is called a nappe.

The Rocky Mountains on the west coast of North America

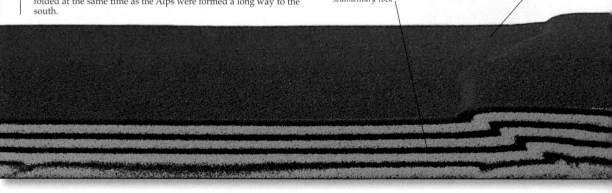

Simple deformation of sedimentary rock

Foothills

MODELLING MOUNTAINS

It is hard to understand how the complicated structures which geologists map in the field have come into being. Simplified models of mountain ranges forming from continental collisions can be made in a laboratory. A machine spreads coloured sand in a tank. A paper sheet is rolled slowly underneath the sand, reducing the length of the layers to imitate subduction (p.43).

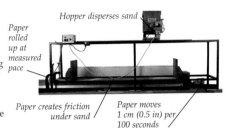

Hopper disperses sand

Paper rolled up at measured pace

Paper creates friction under sand

Paper moves 1 cm (0.5 in) per 100 seconds

Sediments are laid down

First folds

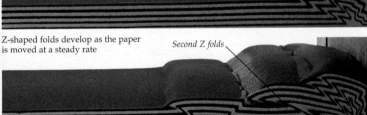

Z-shaped folds develop as the paper is moved at a steady rate

Second Z folds

New folds begin to form; the first set are more intensely deformed

Three nappes created, each underlain by a thrust plane

Nappe

FINAL STAGE

A series of thrusts has placed one nappe on top of another. This model only represents part of what happens in nature. In reality, uplifting, folding, and thrusting are accompanied by erosion, intrusions, and volcanoes.

Nappe

The Andes

There are many signs of continuing uplift and other tectonic activity in the Andes. Many of the world's largest earthquakes originate here. Young marine sediments are found high above sea level, showing that uplift has been rapid. The Andes are distinctive for the large number of active volcanoes which make up many of the highest peaks. These are built above the mountain range itself. The volcanoes have produced great level spreads of ash making up the elevated plateau of the altiplano.

South America

The Andes mountains

MOUNTAINS IN CHILE

The jagged nature of mountains comes about from erosion of land that has been raised by thrusting and deformation in orogenesis.

Continental crust

Mountain range

Sea

Sediments scraped from ocean floor

DESTRUCTIVE PLATE BOUNDARIES

The destructive plate movement in the Andes occurs when oceanic crust subducts beneath the continental crust. Sediments from the ocean floor are scraped off and added to the continent.

Thrust plane

Dictionary check

sedimentary material deposited by water, wind or ice and formed into rock

recrystallized reformed into crystal

deformation the process of altering and changing shape

uplift a lifting up

tectonic relating to structural changes in the earth's crust

plate boundary where two rigid sheets of rock meet in the Earth's crust

What on Earth are freaky peaks?

Strictly speaking, a mountain's a steep-sided rock that rises above the Earth's surface. (Oh, you knew that already?) You measure a mountain by its height above sea level. Even if it's nowhere near the sea. Confusing, eh? Some geographers think proper peaks must be at least 1,000 metres high (that's like three Eiffel Towers plonked on top of each other) if you're going to call them mountains. Others say any old (large-ish) hill or hump will do.

For hundreds of years, mountains had geographers mystified. They knew freaky peaks existed (OK, so you don't have to be a brain surgeon to work that out) but they couldn't agree how they'd got there. Here are some of their over-the-top theories. . .

According to English vicar Thomas Burnet (1635–1715) the Earth's surface was once as smooth as an eggshell. But God wanted to punish people for their sins. So he cracked the shell open and water poured out. (Remember Noah and the Ark? This is the flood that made them famous.) The slivers of smashed-up shell became mountains. It might sound weird to us now. But astonishingly, a hundred years later, Thomas's eggy theory was still going strong.

Meanwhile, top Scottish geographer James Hutton (1726–1797) had other ground-breaking ideas. He reckoned (rightly) that peaks were pushed up over millions of years by natural forces which twisted and bent the rocks. But he couldn't say what these freaky forces were. James wrote his ideas down in a long, boring book called *Theory of the Earth*. Unfortunately, very few people bothered to read it because his writing was so hard to understand. Besides, they liked the flood story better.

And it didn't stop there. American geologist James Dwight Dana (1813–1895) claimed the Earth was once a red-hot ball of soft, squishy rock. As it cooled, it shrank, and its surface went all dry and wrinkly (like skin on cold school custard. Yuk. Or your fingers in the bath.). The wrinkly bits were freaky peaks. Simple as that.

It seemed that every geographer worth his or her salt had something to say. But, guess what? They still couldn't say exactly how mountains were made. Freaky peaks had them well and truly stumped.

Teacher teaser

Forgotten to do your geography homework? Why not sidetrack your teacher with this painful question:

PLEASE, MISS, DO MOUNTAINS GO TO THE DENTIST?

What on Earth are you talking about?

Answer: No, mountains don't go to the dentist. Lucky things. But your question's not as silly as it seems. You see, British geographer Sir George Airy (1801–1892) reckoned mountains were a bit like teeth. Freaky peaks were the bits you see (like your gleaming, pearly-white gnashers giving a cheesy grin). But underneath they'd got huge, long, rocky roots reaching down into the ground (just like the roots that hold your teeth in your jaw and stop them falling out). Had brilliant but barmy Sir George bitten off more than he could chew? No, he was right.

Earth-moving ideas

But it wasn't until 1910 that geographers finally got to the root of the peaky problem. Then brilliant German geographer Alfred Wegener (1880–1930) had a brainwave. He worked out that the Earth's rocky surface (called the crust – that's the bit of the Earth right beneath your feet) wasn't anything to do with eggshells or custard. Thank goodness for that. Nope. Instead, the rock was cracked into lots of pieces, called plates, a bit like crazy paving (only on a seriously gigantic scale). There were seven huge chunks and lots of smaller ones. But get this: the plates didn't stay put in one place all the time. They were constantly on the move.

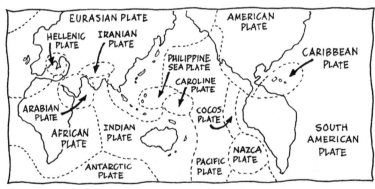

Brainy Alfred called his earth-shattering theory "continental drift". But he couldn't work out what made the plates move. Modern geographers now know the plates float on a layer of hot, gooey rock called magma. It's found underneath the crust (in a layer called the mantle). It's thick and sticky, a bit like treacle. Heat from deep inside the Earth churns up the magma and keeps the crusty plates on their toes.

Normally, the plates drift about without you even noticing. But sometimes, they get in each other's way. Some bash straight into each other. Others try to push and shove their way past. And guess what? Yep, this is how mighty mountains are made. The mystery was over.

From Horrible Geography: Freaky Peaks

 **T** Text level: reading

Information retrieval

1 Read the text from *Eyewitness Science: Earth* carefully. It gives information about:

a) how mountain ranges are formed

b) how people made mistakes in working out how they were formed

c) how different sorts of mountain ranges are created

d) how geologists make models of mountains to work out what's happening.

Find each of these pieces of information in the text (some appear in more than one place) then copy out and complete the following table. The first part of the table is done for you.

Information about	Found under the heading(s)
a) how mountain ranges are formed	Mountain building

2 a) Why did geologists once think that mountain ranges showed that the earth was shrinking?

b) What simile is used to describe that process? Use a quotation from the text to answer this question.

3 Re-read the section headed 'Mountain building'. Which of the following four features do mountain ranges usually have in common?

a) young mountain ranges are always at active plate boundaries

b) foothills are made out of sedimentary rock

c) the middles of mountain ranges have complicated rocks and structures

d) the rocks in the middles of ranges may be deformed and recrystallised.

4 Read closely the section headed 'The Rocky Mountains'. Use quotations to support your answers to the following questions:

   a) What far-fetched idea turned out to be right?

   b) What does the writer suggest would be hard to imagine?

5 Throughout the text from *Eyewitness Science: Earth*, page numbers are given in brackets. Why does the writer do this and what is the reader expected to do?

6 Read the *Freaky Peaks* text closely and compare it to the text from *Eyewitness Science: Earth*. List three similarities that you find between the two texts and three differences. You may wish to consider content, layout and the use of headings and diagrams in your answer.

7 Both texts provide explanations of why there are different types of mountain ranges. In which text was it easier to find this information? Give reasons for your answer.

8 Both texts describe the processes by which mountains are formed.

   a) Who would be the most likely audience for the *Eyewitness Science: Earth* text? When do you think this text would be used?

   b) Who would be the most likely audience for the *Freaky Peaks* text? Give reasons for your answer.

   c) Do you think the texts are successful for their intended audiences? Why?

   Think about:

- the techniques used in each text to present information
- the type of information included in each text
- the balance between text and pictures.

9 Using information from both texts, summarise three mistaken beliefs about how mountains are formed.

W Word level

Joining ideas with connectives

Connectives are the words used to join ideas together in texts in order to present information more clearly. Words as simple as 'and' and 'then' are connectives; as well as less familiar words such as 'nothwithstanding' and 'whereas'. Connectives can be grouped together according to the function that they have.

Example

Connectives can:
indicate time – *'after'*, *'later'*, *'until'*, *'since'*
give reasons – *'because'*, *'so'*, *'therefore'*
indicate purpose – *'to'*, *'so'*, *'as'*

1 a) How many connectives can you identify in the two texts that you have been reading? Write down the ones you can find.

b) Categorise the connectives you have found according to their function. Copy out and complete the following table. The first connective from the *Eyewitness Science* text has been done for you.

Connective used	Function		
	Time	Reasons	Purpose
It is now known ...	*now*		

2 What differences do you notice between the uses the writers have made of connectives in the two texts?

When reading texts in your key stage 3 tests you may come across unfamiliar vocabulary that you find difficult. Both these texts contain vocabulary that is hard to spell, such as 'colossal' and 'sedimentary'.

3 Identify five unfamiliar words from each text, then use the spelling strategy – look, say, cover, write, check – to make sure you can spell these words confidently and accurately.

S Sentence level

Commenting on the writer's use of language

> In your key stage 3 tests you will encounter questions that ask you to comment on the way that writers use language to create different effects. These questions are testing not only your ability to **identify** different features of language used in a text but also to **explain** the effects they create. In order to be successful when answering this type of question there are some important techniques to remember:
>
> * always use quotations in your answer to back up the point you are making
>
> * use short quotations that focus the reader on the language feature you are commenting on
>
> * If you are quoting only part of a sentence, end your quotation with an **ellipsis**: '...'
>
> * always explain your quotation, making sure your explanation helps answer the question.

1 In what ways does the writer of the *Freaky Peaks* text try to keep the reader interested in what is being written about? Think in particular about the writer's use of language.

Write two paragraphs in answer to this question. Use the mini-writing frame on the next page to help you, using quotations to back up the points you make. Techniques you might want to write about in your answer include:

* making jokes to make the information more amusing
* putting comments into brackets
* asking the reader questions to check understanding
* using colloquial, friendly vocabulary.

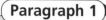

> **Paragraph 1**
>
> In order to hold the reader's interest, the writer of *Freaky Peaks* writes as if she is actually speaking to the reader. For example, the writer states, ' ...' This is exactly how someone who knew you well might speak to you.

> **Paragraph 2**
>
> Another technique the writer uses is ...
> An example of this is '...
> This holds the interest of the reader because ....

SL Speaking and listening

Tailoring your presentation to the right audience

Your school has an open evening to introduce new Year 7 pupils to the school. Your teacher has asked your class to prepare presentations to show the work you have recently completed in class. These presentations should be suitable to be shown to parents and new Year 7 pupils.

Look back at your answer to question 9 in the Text level: reading section on page 45. For your presentation, you are going to demonstrate how well you have understood these complex ideas by explaining them to parents and pupils.

- You may use PowerPoint slides, overhead projector transparencies or a set of posters to explain the mistaken beliefs about how mountains formed. Whichever format you choose, you must also provide a spoken commentary which explains your thinking in detail.

- Work in pairs to create your presentation which should not last longer than three minutes.

When you have completed your presentation, show it to the rest of your class. They should evaluate the presentation, making it clear whether it:

- was suitable for an audience of parents and younger children
- held their interest
- was presented clearly and audibly.

Writing to inform

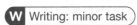
Writing: minor task

Study closely the large central diagrams on page 41 of the *Eyewitness Science* text headed 'Modelling mountains'. The text provides information about how 'folds' are formed in mountain ranges. This information is then clarified by the diagrams.

Choose a word or phrase relating to a hobby, sport, or interest, that you have and write a 50-word paragraph to explain it, backing up your explanation with a carefully-labelled diagram or diagrams.

Writing: major task

You have been asked to produce a chapter for a book in the same series as *Freaky Peaks* entitled 'Horrible ...'. You could write about a subject that you study in school, such as 'Horrible History' or 'Horrible English', or you could choose to write about a 'Horrible Hobby' that you have.

When you have decided on the subject for your horrible chapter, you can then start to plan your writing. Remember – the key to writing in this style is to present complicated material in a way that is interesting and easy to understand.

- First of all, research your chosen subject, gathering the material you will need to write your informative chapter.

- Then create a paragraph plan by writing down the first sentence of every paragraph you intend to include.

- Decide on the headings and sub-headings you are going to use and think about where you will insert diagrams and cartoons.

You should aim to write around 500 words. You may use the writing frame on the next page to help you with your writing.

Heading

- Ask the reader a question.
- Use language that grabs the reader's attention right from the start.

Paragraph one

- Make a statement that answers the question that you asked.
- Follow up with a comment to the reader in brackets, such as 'Oh you knew that already?'

Paragraph two

- Add in more information, again, asking questions and adding in comments as you go.
- Use the second person 'you' to talk to the reader as if they were in the room with you.

Paragraph three

- Try to interest your reader with unusual and interesting facts about your chosen subject.
- Keep your choice of language as close to spoken language as you can.

Paragraph four

- Sum up the information you have provided.
- Try to provide a snappy conclusion.

Help box

1. You should use simple sentences, keeping them mostly short and sharp. Break up more difficult ideas into complex sentences, containing simple, easy-to-understand clauses.

2. Break up the text with diagrams, cartoons and jokes.

Unit 5: Explain

It is easier to **explain** how to do something, such as preparing a recipe, by actually showing someone how to do it, rather than explaining how to do it in writing. But in the nineteenth century the option of showing people how to cook on television didn't exist, and the celebrity chefs of those times had to explain their recipes in writing. In this unit you will get the chance to see how successful the Delia Smith of her day, Mrs Beeton, was at explaining to her readers how to prepare a recipe for beef. You will compare this with the writing of the TV chef, Jamie Oliver, who breaks all the rules of how to set out a recipe in his explanation of how to make an ice-cream dessert called a 'smush in'.

Pre-reading

What differences might you expect to find between the two recipes you are about to read? Remember one was written by a celebrity chef who frequently appears on television, whilst the other was written by a Victorian lady who wrote books of household advice for other Victorian ladies. List three differences that you would expect to find.

Mrs Beeton's Book of Household Management

Beef à la mode

INGREDIENTS

6 or 7 lbs. of the thick flank of beef,
a few slices of fat bacon,
1 teacupful of vinegar,
black pepper, allspice, salt to taste,
2 cloves well mixed and finely pounded, making altogether 1 heaped teaspoonful;
1 bunch of savoury herbs, including parsley, all finely minced and well mixed;
3 onions, 2 large carrots, 1 turnip, 1 head of celery,
1½ pint of water, 1 glass of port wine.

Mode – Slice and fry the onions to a pale brown, and cut up the other vegetables in small pieces, and prepare the beef for stewing in the following manner: choose a fine piece of beef, cut the bacon into long slices, about an inch in thickness, dip them into vinegar, and then into a little of the above seasoning of spice, mixed with the same quantity of herbs. With a sharp knife make holes deep enough to let in the bacon; then rub the beef over the remainder of the seasoning and herbs, and bind it up in a nice shape with tape. Have ready a well-tinned stewpan (it should not be much larger than the piece of meat you are cooking), into which put the beef, with the vegetables, vinegar, and water. Let it simmer *very gently* for 5 hours, or rather longer, should the meat not be extremely tender, and turn it once or twice. When ready to serve, take out the beef, remove the tape, and put it on a hot dish. Skim off every particle of fat from the gravy, add the port wine, just let it boil, pour it over the beef, and it is ready to serve. Great care must be taken that this does *not* boil fast, or the meat will be tough and tasteless; it should only just bubble. When convenient, all kinds of stews should be cooked on a hot-plate, as the process is so much more gradual than on an open fire.

Time – 5 hours, or rather more. *Average cost* – 7d. per lb.
Sufficient for 7 or 8 persons
Seasonable all the year, but more suitable for a winter dish.

From *Mrs Beeton's Book of Household Management*

Happy Days with the Naked Chef

Shopping

When I was as little as five years old, my dad used to take me to the fruit and veg market and to the cash and carry to get the essentials. I honestly used to feel slightly more grown-up and completely honoured when Dad used to say, 'Go on, son, I want you to go and pick me the best box of raspberries. Make sure you taste them, all right', which I used to do with great concentration. He used to have me groping melons, eating apples and sniffing herbs. I would scurry back to Dad with my opinion and some for him to try. Then we'd negotiate a price together and put it all in the van to go back to the pub. Even though I loved it, I think my dad used to take liberties with me being too keen, as he would say, 'Listen to Dad and go and tell that man over there that his fruit and veg is too expensive and a load of old rubbish'. Which I did with great conviction – resulting in me legging it from the warehouse!

So really try to get the kids involved in making some shopping decisions, because all they want is to be treated like grown-ups. Instead of letting them trail behind you while you pile things into the trolley, ask them to choose a pineapple by smelling it to check that it's ripe, for instance. Kids are like sponges – they soak up information and remember everything – so talk to them, ask their opinions on what fish looks good or what meat to try. This can be good fun, especially when you reach the deli counter, as you can try out different things with them. Ask your kids to taste Parma ham, then ask them what they think. No matter what, always let them have some input when out shopping and listen to them seriously. If they realize their opinion counts then they will want to get involved when it comes to cooking the ingredients.

Smush Ins

Smush ins are one of the coolest things to make. I remember when I was a kid, me and my sister would always try to defrost our hard ice-cream in our dessert bowls into almost a thick milkshakey consistency before scoffing the lot. Then as we matured we realized that many flavours could be mushed in to improve the flavour of the rubbishy ice-cream that our parents always used to give us.

So, from the word 'mush' and the phrase 'mushing it in' they became 'smush ins'. It was great going round the supermarkets as a kid, secretly slipping possible smush ins into the trolley. Anything could be a contender – from maple syrup to bashed up chocolate bits, meringue, fruit – you name it, we could smush it! Winegums aren't so good though. But melted chocolate caramel bars are choooooooice.

All you need to do is get a big pot of vanilla ice-cream and a selection of possible smush ins. Take two large scoops of ice-cream per person, blob these on to a clean chopping board, sprinkle or dribble over your flavours and then, with a spatula or fork, mush and smush them together. Scoop up and lob into a bowl or cornet.

Give these a bash and make an event of them when you've got all the kids round. They're really good fun and great to use as bribes to get the kids helping you with the proper cooking! Smush away.

From *Happy Days with the Naked Chef* by Jamie Oliver

Dictionary check

consistency degree of thickness

 **T** Text level: reading

Comparing writers from different times

Questions 1–3 are about the extract from *Mrs Beeton's Book of Household Management.*

1 a) Read the text through carefully then note down five words or phrases that indicate that this is not a modern piece of writing.

b) What word might replace 'mode' in a more modern recipe?

2 a) What are the two most important steps to take in the recipe? How does the writer indicate their importance?

b) What do you think would be the most complicated step to follow in the recipe? Give reasons for your answer.

3 a) Explain what the word 'seasonable' means.

b) What does the timing given for the recipe suggest about the way people prepared food at this time?

Questions 4–6 are about the extract from *Happy Days with the Naked Chef.*

4 a) In what ways did Jamie Oliver's dad get him involved in shopping decisions?

b) Why does Jamie Oliver suggest children need to feel that their opinion of food counts?

5 Explain in your own words what a 'smush in' is and how its name was created.

6 How does Jamie Oliver try to create a friendly and informal relationship with his audience in the text you have read? Use quotations to support your answer, focusing on:

- the writer's choice of vocabulary
- the use of colloquial expressions and informal writing style
- the way punctuation and non-standard English are used.

7 Who do you think the audiences for each of these texts might be? Give reasons for your answer.

8 Both extracts offer explanations, opinions and instructions.

   a) Which text instructs the reader the most? Support your answer with two quotations.

   b) Which text offers the most personal opinion? Again, support your answer with two quotations.

   c) Which text offers the easiest explanations to understand? Explain your answer using quotations from the text.

9 Consider the two recipes you have read. Which would you find easiest to follow and why?

Imperative verbs and their impact on tone

You will be familiar with the use of the term **imperative sentence** – a sentence that gives an instruction. Instructions can be phrased politely and gently: 'Please wait here' or more strongly: Wait please' or very forcefully: 'Wait!', but the form of the verb being used is always the same – the **imperative form**. What changes is the choice of words with which the writer surrounds the verb giving the instruction. These change according to the relationship the writer wishes to establish with the reader – this might be warm and friendly or more formal and severe. Read the following two passages.

a) When ready to serve, take out the beef, remove the tape, and put it on a hot dish. Skim off every particle of fat from the gravy, add the port wine, just let it boil, pour it over the beef, and it is ready to serve.

b) All you need to do is get a big pot of vanilla ice-cream and a selection of possible smush ins. Take two large scoops of ice-cream per person, blob these on to a clean chopping board, sprinkle or dribble over your flavours and then, with a spatula or fork, mush and smush them together. Scoop up and lob into a bowl or cornet.

1 In each passage identify the imperative verbs being used.

2 Explain in your own words what the differences are in tone between the two paragraphs and how these are achieved. Think about the vocabulary used in each paragraph.

3 Now think of three ways in which you might instruct, using the imperative form of the verb, a young child not to cross the road without looking carefully first.

   a) When teaching a child at home about road safety.

   b) When explaining about road safety walking along a pavement.

   c) When the child is just about to run out in front of a vehicle.

4 Jamie Oliver invents two new verbs, 'to smush' and 'to blob'. Can you invent a new verb to describe a process involved in cooking?

Using complex sentences

Although the recipe from *Mrs Beeton's Book of Household Management* may appear harder to understand than the extract from Jamie Oliver's *Happy Days with the Naked Chef*, there are similarities in the ways the two writers construct sentences. Both writers frequently use **complex sentences** to provide several pieces of information. Re-read the following sentences carefully:

a) Slice and fry the onions to a pale brown, and cut up the other vegetables into small pieces, and prepare the beef for stewing in the following manner: choose a fine piece of beef, cut the bacon into long slices, about an inch in thickness, dip them into vinegar, and then into a little of the above seasoning of spice, mixed with the same quantity of herbs.

b) Take 2 large scoops of ice-cream per person, blob these on to a clean chopping board, sprinkle or dribble over your flavours and then, with a spatula or fork, mush and smush them together.

1 Copy out these two sentences and annotate them to show the ways the writers have broken down the information into smaller and more readable chunks. You should comment on:

- the use of punctuation

- the placing of clauses within the sentence.

2 Using either sentence a) or sentence b) as a model, describe how to boil an egg. You must use the same pattern of sentence construction, including punctuation.

3 Briefly explain why you think the writers of recipes use this type of sentence construction. What are the advantages and the disadvantages?

SL Speaking and listening

Devising a script

You have had an idea for a new television programme, which is designed to explain to viewers how to do something. The programme is called 'How to …' and involves a sportsperson, pop star, model, chef, make-up artist or some other celebrity explaining how to carry out a complex task – in just three minutes.

The format of the programme is that the celebrity will show the TV presenter exactly what to do. The role of the TV presenter is to ask the kinds of question that the audience at home might be asking, and to clarify what the celebrity is doing throughout the demonstration.

You are going to work in a pair. First of all, decide on the content of your three-minute programme and which celebrity you will choose to appear in it. Then you should move on to create the script for the programme. Your aims are to work together to:

- Write a script which clearly explains to the audience exactly what they would have to do. You could explain how to score a penalty, how to apply lip-liner, how to change a car tyre, how to cook a particular dish, and so on.

- Script what the celebrity will say and also what the TV presenter will say in response. Remember the role of the TV presenter is to ask questions and to clarify what is going on.

- Keep your audience entertained for three minutes – they need to learn exactly what to do but this information should be presented in an interesting way.

When you have completed your script, try it out on another pair of pupils and ask them to comment on how well it meets the aims listed above.

Writing to explain

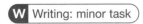 Writing: minor task

You are now going to write up the script for the television programme 'How to …' that you devised in the Speaking and listening activity. You should make any necessary changes to your script in the light of the feedback you received from the pupils that you presented it to.

Include in the script details of where the celebrity and the TV presenter will be standing and what they will be doing as the programme progresses. You could include details of the studio set and the equipment that will be needed. You may also include suggestions about camera angles and lighting if you wish.

 Writing: major task

Throughout key stage 3 you have been learning how writers can shift between genres in a single piece of writing. This is seen very clearly in the extract from *Happy Days with the Naked Chef* by Jamie Oliver. This text is part autobiography and part explanation, but also includes lots of descriptive writing and information too.

You are now going to write an autobiographical essay, which also includes, as Jamie Oliver's writing does, explanations and advice. Think back to a time when you were being taught how to do something – it doesn't matter what. It might be learning to ride a bicycle, learning to swim, or learning to speak a foreign language. You should base your autobiographical essay on this experience and include explanations and advice so that others could learn to do the same thing successfully.

Use the writing frame on the next page to help you structure your writing.

How I learned to …

First section

- Describe the experience in detail. You will find it easiest to write about if you describe just a small part of this experience rather than trying to describe it all.

- Explain not only what you learned but also how you learned it.

- You might want to include information about who taught you and your thoughts and feelings about the experience.

- Think about your choice of vocabulary and the use of colloquial expressions to build up an informal relationship with the reader.

Second section

- You should include advice to your readers about how best to learn for themselves how to do what you did.

- Use your experience to focus this advice. You might want to focus on the lessons that can be learned from mistakes you made or successes you had.

- You should include imperative sentences and think carefully about your choice of words surrounding the imperative form of the verb. Make sure you maintain an appropriate tone.

Final section

- Offer clear instructions for how your readers might carry out the activity themselves.

- Keep this section simple and uncomplicated, offering straightforward guidance which would have been of use to you when you were learning.

- Use a variety of simple and complex sentences.

- Think about the order in which you place clauses in the sentence and the punctuation you use to break the explanation into readily understandable chunks.

Unit 6: Describe

Writers can make memorable occasions come alive for their readers by vividly recreating the atmosphere and action of the moment through their use of **description**. Some writers will focus on the drama of the occasion and use vocabulary which reflects the colour, movement and tension; others may choose to concentrate on the personal element, showing what the occasion means to an individual or to themselves.

You are going to read two accounts of the 2002 World Cup Final between the Brazilian and German football teams. One of the reports is from the *Daily Mirror* and was published the day after the final, whilst the other is an extract from an online commentary, which was broadcast on the Internet as the match was actually happening. Before you read, think about a major sporting occasion or other spectacular event which captured your imagination and interest. Write down words and phrases which vividly convey the atmosphere of the occasion.

FIFA WORLD CUP 2002 KOREA JAPAN THE FINA

THIS time he was on the team-sheet from the start. This time he was his real self. This time the fairytale came true.

Who says that there is no romance left in football?

There is no better story than one man's resurrection, taking the chance to send every possible bad memory hurtling into the abyss, never to be dwelled upon again.

Darkness had long fallen on the Land of the Rising Sun, but Yokohama was lit up last night by the buck-toothed smile football feared it would never see again.

Four years ago in the Stade de France, assailed by mental and physical doubts, Ronaldo was a wreck – present in body but not in spirit.

Yet finally, after all that has happened in the intervening period, the Brazilian was able to put the past to bed.

on the spot when the German skipper spilled Rivaldo's shot at his feet.

Three times earlier in the match, something – maybe nerves, perhaps just Kahn's brilliance, possibly simply fate, appeared to be conspiring against him again.

Yet this time, as the ball slipped from Kahn's shovel-hands, there was only one possible outcome, the net billowing in an instant.

Germany may not agree, but the rest of us should give thanks that he did come back from the anguish of Paris, the hell of those knee injuries.

In Yokohama, we saw once again what might have been and what hopefully will be for the next years to come.

The Germans were left to blame themselves. Kahn for this one mistake of the tournament, Didi Haman for being robbed by Ronaldo in the build-up.

Yet this was a victory for attack over defence, for the team that deserved to win its nation their fifth World Cup crown.

Yet not without problems.

It had been billed as Kahn against the Three R's. But with Rivaldo going missing in action it was not quite like that, even though the best outfield player in the German squad, Michael Ballack, was forced to watch the Final from the bench following his ill-timed suspension.

Until Kahn's fatal slip, which came after he had damaged his finger saving from Gilberto Silva, he had lived up to the form that had brought Germany so far, as Rudi Voller's side stuck to their gameplan.

Whenever the Brazilians tried to dwell on the ball, the tackles came snapping in, Jens Jeremies, Hamann, Bernd Schneider and Thomas Linke flying in to win the ball.

It worked to frustrate and for long periods neutralise Brazil, whose best work came from Ronaldinho and Kleberson.

But while Voller had targeted the space

As he ran to all parts of the Yokohama International Stadium, mobbed by photographers and teammates alike, every soul-searching second of those four years was left trailing behind him.

This was redemption in its most intense form.

Two goals on the biggest stage that distanced him from the nightmares and the agony, the pain and the suffering.

That it should have been Oliver Kahn, the man almost single-handedly responsible for bringing Germany to Yokohama, who effectively handed Brazil their fifth World Cup was one of football's bitter ironies.

But when it mattered, "King Kahn" was dethroned by the true monarch of football, the man who was born to be

MATCH STATS
GERMANY v BRAZIL

0	GOALS	2
3	SHOTS ON TARGET	6
7	SHOTS OFF TARGET	3
9	BLOCKED SHOTS	2
13	CORNERS	3
22	FOULS CONCEDED	19
1	OFFSIDES	0
0	RED CARD	0
1	YELLOW CARDS	1
58	POSSESSION %	42
72	PASSING ACCURACY %	70
88	TACKLE SUCCESS %	70

REPRODUCED FROM THE opta index

How he won Golden Boot

8: Ronaldo (Bra); 5: Klose (Ger) Rivaldo (Bra); 4: Tomasson (Den) Vieri (It); 3: Ballack (Ger) Diop (S'gal) Keane (Ire) Larsson (Sw) Mansiz (Tur) Morientes (Sp) Pauleta (Por) Raul (Sp) Wilmots (Bel); 2: Borgetti (Mex) Camara (S'gal) Cuevas (Par) Davala (Tur) Donovan (US) Gomez (C Rica) Hierro (Sp) Inamoto (Jap) Jung-hwan (SKor) McBride (US) Owen (Eng) Ronaldinho (Bra) Sas (Tur).

How Ronaldo struck gold

CAFU lifts the World Cup, but it was Ronaldo who ensured he would get his hands on it with these two goals. His first (left) came when Oliver Khan could only parry Rivaldo's fierce shot, and Ronaldo's precise finish (above) clinched it.

Dictionary check

redemption the act of being made free of blame and brought back into favour
the Three Rs the nickname given to the group of Brazilian footballers – Ronaldo, Rivaldo and Ronaldhino

mirrorsport@mgn.co.uk **DAILY MIRROR**, *Monday, July 1, 2002* PAGE 63

GERMANY 0 BRAZIL 2 FROM YOKOHAMA

IT'S THE TWO RONNIES

Ronaldo's double ends a four-year nightmare.. and puts him back on top of the world

Martin Lipton
CHIEF FOOTBALL WRITER

SHOUT OF THIS WORLD: Smiling Ronaldo celebrates after laying the ghost of France 98 to rest in emphatic style

behind Cafu and Roberto Carlos as the opportunities for his team to exploit, they lacked the attacking thrust to make the most of that.

Crosses

Twice, once down each flank, Schneider made ground into penetrating positions, but with only Miroslav Klose to aim for his crosses were cut out.

Brazil were not functioning smoothly, but every so often broke free to cut huge holes in the German rearguard.

The chances came, but were not taken, with Ronaldo initially the guiltiest man.

In the 18th minute Gilberto Silva dashed up the left to find Ronaldinho. His pass, cutting out Carsten Ramelow and Christoph Metzelder, was perfect but it seemed as if Ronaldo was too concerned at Kahn's looming presence. Instead of doing what should have come naturally and finding the net, he limply pushed wide with the outside of his left foot.

Brazil were not helped by Rivaldo's stunningly insignificant contribution, although Germany still had Kahn to thank for remaining on terms at the interval.

The skipper stood up long enough to gather as Ronaldo stretched to get contact on Ronaldinho's lobbed pass and also put Kleberson off as he dragged wide.

The pressure was building and the 60 seconds before the break intensified that feeling.

Ronaldinho zipped down the left and Ronaldo's dummy saw the ball run to Kleberson, whose curling right-footer beat Kahn's dive but thudded back off the bar, landing outside the box.

Germany did not regroup and when Roberto Carlos drilled in from the left, the rebound off Metzelder fell for Ronaldo who shot instantly on the turn, only to be foiled once again as Kahn stuck out his right leg. Fortunate to survive, but if Germany were going to upset the odds, they had to ride their luck and take advantage. Twice in the space of four minutes at the start of the second period, they had that opportunity.

First, Neuville's corner found Jeremies unmarked for a free header which hit Edmilson.

Then Neuville lined up a 35-yard free-kick which sped past the wall and was heading for the top corner only for Marcos' right hand to deflect it against the upright and away.

The best chance fell just after the hour, Schneider spinning inside from the right and threading through for Neuville, who needed only to make contact to steer home.

Yet the Leverkusen striker made contact only with the ground, missing the ball altogether and slapping the grass in frustration and annoyance.

It was the pivotal moment. Within four minutes, Ronaldo caught Hamann in possession 15 yards outside his own box, spun on the spot and slipped to Rivaldo, whose shot looked easy-meat.

But Kahn's blunder sent the game on its irrecoverable course, Ronaldo seizing the opportunity and taking the World Cup with him.

Voller tried to change things, sending on Oliver Bierhoff and Gerald Asamoah in an attempt to give his side more firepower.

Asamoah's defensive shortcomings were far more influential 12 minutes from time.

Rivaldo's dummy from Kleberson's pass was bought by Linke, with the substitute caught the wrong side of the ball as Ronaldo coolly stroked into the bottom corner of Kahn's net from 14 yards.

Joy unconfined. Game over, World Cup over, the nightmare over.

While Bierhoff, in his final international game, forced a diving save from Marcos, the die was cast in Brazil's favour.

And rightly so. The best team had won. The best player had won it for them. The perfect end.

BRAZIL: Marcos; Lucio, Edmilson, Roque Junior, Cafu, Gilberto Silva, Kleberson, Roberto Carlos, Rivaldo, Ronaldinho (Juninho 85), Ronaldo, (Denilson 90).

GERMANY: Kahn; Frings, Ramelow, Linke, Metzelder, Schneider, Hamann, Jeremies (Asamoah 76), Bode (Ziege 84), Klose (Bierhoff 73), Neuville.

GERMANY v BRAZIL, TOMORROW, K
THE REBIRTH OF RONALDO
We're a team of many stars, the pressure's off and I'm not even thinking about '98
SATURDAY'S Mirror prediction came true

RETURN OF THE BEAUTIFUL GAME: OLIVER HOLT, PAGES 60 & 61

From the *Daily Mirror*

Online commentary

ONLINE COMMENTARY

World Cup Final 2002

Frings looks for Bode: Germany come forward again with Jeremies and his shot deflects wide for a corner [69 min]

Marcos flips it away, and Germany keep the pressure up to win another corner [70 min]

That comes to nothing: a free-kick is given for a foul as Brazil defend the set piece [71 min]

Great run by Lucio – he motors into the area and crosses, but it eludes the waiting Ronaldo [72 min]

Change for Germany: Klose is off and Oliver Bierhoff comes on as boss Voller tries to refresh his side [72 min]

Jeremies looks for the substitute, who then looks to Neuville … [73 min]

Frings hits a shot and is rewarded with a corner as the ball deflects away [74 min]

Neuville plays it in and Roque Junior heads it clear for Brazil [75 min]

Hamann tries a long-range free-kick; Brazil block, but Germany are turning up the pressure now … [76 min]

… until Bierhoff is penalised for a foul, and Brazil grab the chance to move forward. Jeremies goes off and Gerald Asamoah comes on in another Germany switch [76 min]

Asamoah's into the action again quickly, challenging Roberto Carlos down the left … but here come Brazil again [77 min]

Cafu feeds Ronaldo just inside the area and the finish is cool, calm and perfect. It's 2–0 Brazil – surely they are world champions now! [78 min]

Sublime finishing from, surely, the player of the tournament … he's got eight goals overall now. Dazzling stuff [79 min]

From ESPN

 Text level: reading

Reporting facts and presenting opinions

1 Re-read the first section of the *Daily Mirror* report from 'This time he was on the team-sheet …' to 'Yet not without problems.' The report begins by focusing on the importance of the occasion to one man, Ronaldo.

  a) What facts are included in this section which explain why the occasion might have been so important to him?

  b) Why do you think the writer uses the metaphor 'one man's resurrection'?

  c) Why do you think the writer says so much about Ronaldo before reporting the events of the game?

2 What evidence does the writer of the *Daily Mirror* report give that German mistakes contribute to their defeat? Pick out quotations from the text to support your answer.

> Sometimes writers of newspaper reports will mix their own opinions with the factual reporting of an occasion or event. The **facts** which are given will be unarguable; they can be proven to be true.
>
> **Example**
>
> > *Ronaldo scored both goals.*
>
> **Opinions** are what one person thinks and cannot be proven to be true. Opinions are therefore subjective or personal judgements.
>
> **Example**
>
> > *The best team had won it.*
>
> We might agree with the above statement, but it is open to argument. Including facts makes the description more believable, whilst incorporating opinions challenges the reader to consider their own view of the situation.

3 Look again at the two paragraphs of the *Daily Mirror* report from 'That it should have been Oliver Kahn …' to ' … spilled Rivaldo's shot at his feet.'

a) Draw a table with two columns, one headed 'Fact' and the other headed 'Opinion' and list the information from these paragraphs in the relevant columns.

b) How many facts are contained in the paragraphs and how many opinions? Why do you think this is?

c) Briefly explain what this leads you to think about the reliability of the information in the report.

4 In the online commentary, it says of Ronaldo '… sublime finishing from, surely, the player of the tournament' whereas the *Daily Mirror* report states 'The best player had won it for them.'

a) List the factual evidence from both texts which supports the view that Ronaldo was 'the best player of the tournament'.

b) Is there any evidence which challenges this view? Pick out quotations from the text.

5 Re-read the closing section of the *Daily Mirror* report from 'Voller tried to change things …' to the end of the article. Then read the online commentary which deals with the same passage of play.

a) Copy out and complete the following table. List the information given in each account and show where their descriptions of the action agree and disagree.

The *Daily Mirror*	Online commentary	Similarities and differences
Voller tried to change things, sending on Oliver Bierhoff and Gerald Asamoah.	*Klose is off and Oliver Bierhoff comes on as boss Voller tries to refresh his side 72 mins*	*The Daily Mirror implies that both substitutions took place at the same time. The online commentary states that they happened at different times.*

b) Write a short analysis of the reports, evaluating the fullness and accuracy of the information they provide.

Word level

Extended metaphors and emotive vocabulary

Commentaries and newspaper reports of sporting events often use language which normally we might associate with another activity or situation to convey the drama and action of the contest being described. The *Daily Mirror* report makes extensive use of language associated with military matters.

Example

- *Rivaldo going missing in action ...*
- *... huge holes in the German rearguard.*
- *... more firepower.*

This frequent use of language associated with warfare helps to establish a metaphor and develop it through the text. This is called an **extended metaphor** and its use in these texts creates a sense of the World Cup Final almost as a battle.

1 What other examples of language associated with warfare can you find in the *Daily Mirror* report? Pick out quotations from the text.

2 Find examples of language associated with other areas, such as religion, which are used in the *Daily Mirror* report. Explain why you think the writer has used these extended metaphors.

3 a) Rewrite the first four sentences of the online commentary, making use of language which is associated with warfare to create your own extended metaphor.

b) Briefly explain what effect you feel you have created by doing this.

4 Rewrite the same four sentences using vocabulary associated with the following areas to create different effects:

a) chess

b) theatre

c) boxing.

5 Write a brief commentary on what you feel have been the effects of the changes you have made in the rewritten versions.

> The writers of the newspaper report and the online commentary both include **emotive vocabulary**. This is vocabulary selected specifically to appeal to the feelings and provoke a response in the reader.
>
> Example
>
> > *In the online commentary Ronaldo's second goal is described as '**sublime** finishing' and '**dazzling** stuff'.*
>
> These adjectives help to create the sense that the goal was a breathtaking experience.

6 a) Read closely the online commentary to pick out examples of emotive vocabulary. Categorise these into nouns, verbs, adjectives and adverbs.

b) Explain which examples of the vocabulary you have listed you feel is the most effective and give your reasons.

c) Write an online commentary for the scoring of the first goal. Use some of the emotive vocabulary you have identified and any other emotive vocabulary you feel is appropriate.

S Sentence level

The rule of three

> Writers often use the **rule of three** to emphasise important points in many types of writing, but it is often thought of as an effective technique to use in descriptive writing. A writer's control of the punctuation and sentence structures used can add to the impact of this technique.
>
> Example
>
> > *This time he was on the team-sheet from the start. This time he was his real self. This time the fairytale came true.*

1 Look carefully at the opening three sentences of the *Daily Mirror* report. What do you think is the impact of opening the report in this way? You should comment on:

- the length and structure of the sentences
- how effectively they involve the reader.

2 Scan the rest of the report to find two other examples of the use of the rule of three. Comment on the effectiveness of each example.

3 Rewrite the opening paragraph of the *Daily Mirror* report as one sentence, using commas and connectives to separate the clauses. Then write a sentence evaluating what you think is the effect of the change.

> The rule of three can by used by writers in a variety of ways, such as layering adjectives for emphatic effect.
>
> Example
>
> > *Cafu feeds Ronaldo just inside the area and the finish is* **cool**, **calm** and **perfect**.
>
> The effect of the use of the rule of three here is to emphasise the control and precision of Ronaldo's play.
>
> Writers can also experiment with the rule of three and even break the rule as this sentence from the *Daily Mirror* report shows.
>
> Example
>
> > *Two goals on the biggest stage that distanced him from the* **nightmares** *and the* **agony**, *the* **pain** *and the* **suffering**.
>
> The rule of three has been broken here by creating pairs of **abstract nouns** to intensify the contrast between the pain of Ronaldo's past and the joy of his present performance.

4 Re-read the final section of the *Daily Mirror* report from 'Joy unconfined' to the end of the report.

a) Explain how the writer uses the rule of three in this section and what effect this has on the reader.

b) Rewrite this section by experimenting with the rule of three and explain the effect you have achieved by doing so.

Becoming a football commentator

Working in a pair, you are going to script and present football commentaries on the 2002 World Cup Final. One of you will take on the role of a Brazilian radio commentator, the other the role of a German radio commentator. Clearly their viewpoints on the match will be somewhat different.

You are going to prepare short commentaries based on the build-up to and the scoring of the first Brazilian goal. Look back at the *Daily Mirror* report to remind yourself of what happened and copy and complete this planning frame to help organise your script.

Action	German commentator	Brazilian commentator
Play leading up to the first goal	*Could comment on Hamman's mistake in losing the ball*	*Might focus on Ronaldo's tackle to rob Hamman of the ball*
Rivaldo's shot		
Ronaldo's follow-up shot		
Reaction of the crowd		
Reaction of the players		

When you start to script and practise the commentaries in your pair, you should:

• try to focus on the pace and excitement of the match
• show how the advantage swings from one team to the other through changes in your tone of voice
• alternate the commentaries to show the different commentators' views of the same event.

When you have completed your radio commentaries, you could record them using a tape recorder and play your performance back to the rest of the group.

Writing to describe

 Writing: minor task

You are a picture editor on a busy tabloid newspaper and have been asked to select and write captions for five photographs to accompany the match report of the World Cup Final. First look back at the photographs on pages 62–63 which accompany the *Daily Mirror* report. Think about the photographs that have been selected and try to decide why they were considered appropriate. Some of them have headings and captions which help to enhance the impact of the image. Look at the ways in which these captions are written.

Use the Internet or any other available resources to find photographs of the 2002 World Cup Final. Select the five images which you think would be most suitable for a tabloid newspaper report of the match and write the captions to accompany each one. You should:

- try to make the captions short and snappy

- think about your use of descriptive language to reflect the action shown in the phototgraph

- think about using puns and humorous references.

 Writing: major task

Look back at your Pre-reading activity on page 61 where you thought about a major sporting occasion or other spectacular event. You are going to write a newspaper report of this event which creates a vivid impression of the occasion for the reader.

Use the writing frame on the next page to help you to structure your report.

What you could include

- Give the context of the occasion.
- Explain where, when and why it is happening.

- Describe the location before the event begins.

- Concentrate on describing key moments of the action.
- Focus on the actions of the participants and the reactions of the spectators.

- Conclude your report by describing the climax of the event.
- Contrast the atmosphere at the start of the event with the mood now.

How you could write it

- **You could use the rule of three by repeating short sentence structures for emphasis.**
- **Try to involve the reader immediately.**

- **Try to create a sense of the atmosphere by including references to colours, sounds and movement.**
- **Introduce an appropriate metaphor here which you can extend by revisiting it throughout the report.**

- **You might want to include some of the words from the Pre-reading activity.**
- **Think about the way your choice of words can show your opinion of certain events.**
- **Use emotive vocabulary to create a sense of the drama of the occasion.**

- **Try to echo the techniques you used in the opening of your report.**
- **Think about how the emotive vocabulary you choose can show how the mood has changed.**

Help box

1. Remember to choose an appropriate headline for your report.
2. Use subheadings to organise your report into sections.

Sn5 Shape paragraphs rapidly

Being able to write in clear, well-organised paragraphs is a skill that you will need for the key stage 3 Writing test.

Your friend has written an article about healthy eating for the school magazine. Unfortunately the school office ended up shredding it. All you have left are three sub-headings: Eat well – stay fit; Fight off coughs and colds; Stay looking better for longer. You are going to work with a partner to reconstruct the shredded article into paragraphs.

▶ Look for opening sentences (in red) which link to the sub-headings

▶ Then look for supporting evidence and examples (in blue) that back up the opening sentences

▶ Finally look for closing sentences (in black) which round off the paragraphs and link each paragraph with the one that follows.

Why does eating matter when it comes to coughs and colds and all the other things we all catch in the winter? Well, eating properly won't stop you being zapped by a cold virus.

There are other bonuses too, quite apart from being healthier. Top models all know that its really important to drink lots of water. This purifies the system, leaving skin clearer, preventing those tired, thirsty headaches many people have by the end of the day.

When you are a teenager it is all too easy to live on a diet of crisps and soft drinks and still feel fit and healthy.

If you want to get fit, though, you have to start taking your eating seriously. Just as you can't run a car without fuel, you can't start to get fit unless you are eating a healthy, balanced diet.

But eating fruit and vegetables pumps up your immune system. You might still get the cold – but you will get better more quickly.

Stopping smoking is the key to a lot of this, too. Long-term smokers have yellowed skin; but if you have stopped smoking, the quickest way back to healthy skin is to eat fruit and vegetables.

People who eat well in their early life will tend to stay looking good much longer – and without the need for the plastic surgery!

So remember – it doesn't have to mean giving up everything you enjoy eating, but having a balanced and healthy diet will make you look better, feel better and perhaps even live longer.

And the really good thing is that by getting fitter you'll start to avoid all those colds that really bring you down in the winter months.

Persuade, argue, advise

In this section you are going to study three very powerful forms of writing: writing to persuade, argue and advise. If the writers of the texts you will encounter in this section are successful, they will change their readers' lives. The writer of a persuasive text sets out to convince a reader to alter their opinion or to do something differently; the writer who presents an argument tries to win a case and make the reader believe what he or she believes; the writer who advises wants the reader to act on this advice.

The writers of each of the texts you will read in the next three units are clear about their purpose and understand very well the needs of their audiences. In most cases they will have carried out detailed research about their audience before they write, because they have to be able to predict and anticipate counter-arguments and to understand thoroughly what will and won't appeal to their audience.

Writers of persuasive texts often choose language to emphasise the positive features of the subject. The Oxfam leaflet you will study uses language that emphasises how challenging and rewarding volunteer work can be, because the writer is aiming to **persuade** the kind of person who is keen to try out new things to give up their time to help Oxfam. Writers of texts that **argue** a particular point of view often use language to challenge the reader. In Unit 8, the writer who wants readers to reject the idea of introducing identity cards uses language that is designed to provoke his readers into action, for example by exaggerating the drawbacks of such a scheme; whereas writers who offer **advice** often use reassuring language, deliberately keeping it simple so that the advice is easily understood.

As you study the texts in these units, you will see that writing to persuade, argue and advise is often bright, lively and interesting. However passionately a writer may feel about an issue, if they can't keep the reader reading they may as well give up. So look out for interesting information, eye-catching layout, jokes, snappy writing and writers who really make their readers think.

Unit 7: Persuade

Writing can be a powerful tool for **persuading** readers to behave or think differently. An effective writer will use a wide range of techniques which are carefully designed to influence a target audience. This is happening around you all the time, particularly in advertisements. As writers and readers you need to be aware of how persuasive writing works.

You are going to read two leaflets published by the charity Oxfam. In both cases, the writers are trying to persuade you to give something – your money or your time. Think about these texts from the points of view of both the writers and the readers. What are the writers doing to try to persuade you to commit your time and money? As readers, how do you respond? Before you read, make a mind-map of the words you associate with Oxfam. What do these words tell you about what you know and how you think about Oxfam now?

Four hours spent in an Oxfam shop will pay for enough vaccinations to immunise twelve children against six diseases.

If you want to start a valuable partnership with Oxfam, and give us some of your spare time, you can get in touch with the Volunteering Team on: **01865 313405**, or **givetime@oxfam.org.uk** or, for shop enquiries, contact your local Shop Manager:

Oxfam
Volunteering for Oxfam: time well spent

Kamna

❝I loved working in a busy shop. There was always something different to do, and so many interesting people to chat to. Everyone who came into the shop made me feel special – they knew I was volunteering my time and how important that was for Oxfam. ❞

Kamna Provost used to volunteer in an Oxfam shop in London. She now has a full-time job with Oxfam.

Peter

❝I'd always wanted to get involved with a large international charity, and Oxfam seemed the obvious choice. Oxfam relies on people who give up their time – this week alone I have helped to pay for enough seeds for a family in Malawi to grow a year's supply of food. ❞

Peter Hobbs is a graduate and works in the Internal Communications Department at Oxfam's Headquarters.

Marie and Elsie

❝I've worked in this shop for 15 years and I still enjoy it. Elsie joined shortly before me, and we've become very good friends. The hours suit me, and I know that even just a few hours of my time can help to pay for a vital medical kit for a midwife in India. ❞

Marie (right) & Elsie have worked in the same shop in Oxford for 15 years. They do just about everything.

At Oxfam we will make the very best use of your time – channelling your skills, ideas, and energy into a wide range of activities. There are lots of different ways you can help – in our shops or offices, or by helping to raise funds, or campaign on an issue that affects the rights of poor people. There's even a graduate-placement scheme designed specially for students who want to gain experience while they decide on a career.

So take a closer look, and surprise yourself.

For nearly 60 years, Oxfam has worked hand-in-hand with poor communities, helping them to make lasting improvements to their lives, from building wells to planting drought-resistant crops. Oxfam's success is made possible by teamwork – by the support of our staff and our donors, and by the invaluable contribution of our volunteers.

Every year, more than 23,000 people give up some of their precious spare time to work for Oxfam – time that allows Oxfam to continue its work with poor communities around the world. This remarkable contribution is based on a partnership that starts from the moment someone agrees to help.

Time spent with Oxfam is definitely time well spent. It will renew your confidence, refresh your skills, provide valuable work experience, and give you the satisfaction of knowing that you are helping poor people to change their lives.

From Monday to Friday, 9am to 5pm, Kieran Battles has a very busy and demanding job. But in his spare time, Kieran is a volunteer for Oxfam. Kieran recently won a competition to visit Oxfam-supported projects in Tanzania, including the Uhuru Primary School.

❝ Time spent with Oxfam definitely changes lives. The teacher there thanked me for giving the children a chance to improve their lives. She was actually thanking everyone who had ever given time to Oxfam. ❞

The Big Sell
Working in an Oxfam Shop

More than £10 million was raised by Oxfam shops last year – shops that are run almost entirely by volunteers.* Oxfam shops are part of the local community, and for many people they are the 'face' of Oxfam. Each shop has its own personality, but they all have the same goal – to **raise money** by selling second-hand books, clothes, and household goods. Many shops also sell a range of Fair Trade foods and crafts. As a shop volunteer, you will have the opportunity to try a variety of tasks, from customer service to keeping accounts and managing the stock. You can arrange the hours and days that suit you, and you'll get plenty of **training and support.** You'll also meet a great bunch of people.

(* financial year 1999-2000)

Money talks
Fundraising for Oxfam

Raising money for Oxfam can be hard work, but it's also **lots of fun.** You can get involved in one of Oxfam's official events and get support from other Oxfam volunteers and staff. Or you can **organise your own event** and experience a sense of real achievement. Why not hold a jumble sale, or organise a sponsored fun-run? Whatever you decide, Oxfam will help you every step of the way.

Taming technology
Working in Oxfam's offices

Oxfam has many busy offices, which always need support from volunteers with computer or administrative skills. If you live in Oxford, or near one of our regional offices, this could be an ideal opportunity for you to gain some valuable experience. Oxfam also runs a **Graduate-Placement Scheme,** which offers students and graduates the chance to gain experience and **skills** in a wide range of work. In return for a commitment of three to five days per week, we can offer you the opportunity to manage a challenging and rewarding project.

Speaking out
Campaigning for Oxfam

These days, people-power counts. Over the years Oxfam has proved that, with the right backing from our volunteers and supporters, major change *is* possible. The international ban on landmines was a huge victory for ordinary people who voiced their anger and concern about the issue. And Fair Trade products, such as *Cafédirect* coffee, are now on sale in most well-known supermarkets. **Your voice definitely counts.** So if you want to be involved in changing history – and people's lives – we can team you up with Oxfam's campaigning network.

MAKE A GIFT FOR LIFE

Oxfam

"My greatest wish would be that water is always available."
Hadija Ibrahim Gido, Sudan

Toby Adamson / Oxfam

Your £2 a month could help

supply clean, safe water for life

keep children healthy
In Bangladesh, just £2 a month could train two volunteer health workers to teach mothers how to safeguard their children from fatal water-borne diseases

Samantha Magee / Oxfam

feed a village
In Zimbabwe, just £2 a month could buy drought-resistant seeds, so that families can grow enough to feed themselves and give their children a brighter future

Calvin Dondo / Oxfam

build wells
In Bolivia, just £2 a month could provide the tools to help people to build wells and give their whole community a permanent supply of clean, safe, drinking water

Julio Etchart/Oxfam

make a difference
Millions more people urgently need your help to build a future free from poverty. A regular gift from you can make a lasting difference to them.

It's simple to help. Just complete the form inside and make your gift today.

THANK YOU

Oxfam

X000BC

Oxfam
Freepost (OF353)
274 Banbury Road
Oxford
OX 7ZS

YOUR GIFT OF £2
A MONTH WILL MAKE
A WORLD OF DIFFERENCE

∨

Just £2 a month from you can make the difference

"Dirty water led to malaria, swelling of legs and limbs, skin diseases and allergies. Cholera and diarrhoea killed our children."
Garinge Somulu, Kouthalam village, India

"Since we built the well and began to cultivate the land, my grandchildren have had enough to eat and they are healthy."
Garinge Somulu, Kouthalam village, India

Rajanikant Yadav / Oxfam

"To get water, we'd leave at midnight one night, and not return until midnight the next day. The water would last two days and then we'd have to go again."
Howa Fudull, Marsus village, Sudan

"Now Oxfam has helped us to get water nearby we can rest, and I have more time to do farming and herding."
Howa Fudull, Marsus village, Sudan

Toby Adamson / Oxfam

"We took samples from the river and they were bad. All the rivers and streams we tested contained cholera – all."
Yona Baringa, water engineer, Uganda

"With the water from the tapstands there's been no cholera in our camp, not one case during the outbreak."
Joyce Masika, Kaburere refugee camp, Uganda

Geoff Sayer / Oxfam

It's amazing what just £2 a month from you could do

Five million people die needlessly each year as a result of water-borne diseases. Yet just £2 a month from you could help to supply a community with clean, safe water for life. In Sudan for example, just £2 a month could pay for the vital tools that drought-stricken villages need to keep their water supplies working throughout the year.

It's simple to help. Just fill in the Regular Giving Form and send your gift today.

This is a self-seal envelope. Tear at perforation, moisten gummed strips, fold, seal, and send.

moisten here

YES, I want to make a regular gift to Oxfam

REGULAR GIVING FORM (Banker's Order)

Please complete details in the Banker's Order Form and return to:
Oxfam, FREEPOST (OF 353), 274 Banbury Road, Oxford, OX2 7ZS

2001QBC003

Title (Mr/Mrs/Miss/Ms)

Full name

Address

Postcode

Please pay Oxfam the sum of

£2 ☐ Other
further notice and debit

each month until

My Account No.

Bank Sort Code –

Starting on (date) / /2001

Please allow at least one month between signing the form and the date of the first payment.

Signature

☐ Please tick here if you would like Oxfam to reclaim the tax that you have paid on all your donation(s) since 6th April 2000 and any future donation(s) you may make. *

To: The Manager (Branch name and address)

Postcode

This cancels all existing Banker's Orders to Oxfam: **Yes / No / N/A**

My Email address is:
Contacting you by e-mail may save Oxfam money. If you prefer not to be contacted in this way please tick here ☐

From time to time, we agree with other like-minded organisations to write to some of each other's supporters for the mutual benefit of both. If you prefer not to be contacted in this way, please tick this box ☐

* In order for Oxfam to reclaim the tax you have paid on your donation(s) you must have paid income or capital gains tax equal to the tax that will be claimed (currently 28p for each £1 you give).

FOR OFFICIAL USE ONLY:
To National Westminster Bank plc, 32 Cornmarket St, Oxford OX1 3HQ (54-21-23), a/c 0855 0999 quoting our reference:

Founded in 1942, Oxfam works with poor people regardless of race or religion in their struggle against hunger, disease, exploitation and poverty.
Oxfam GB is a member of Oxfam International.
Registered charity No. 202918.

Oxfam

moisten here

Audience and purpose

1 Skim-read the leaflets and note down your impressions under the following headings:

▶ *Purpose:* What do the writers want you to do as a result of reading these leaflets?

▶ *Audience:* What clues can you find about the kind of people at whom these leaflets are aimed? Look at the pictures as well as the words.

▶ *Structure:* What information do these leaflets give you? What decisions have the writers made about the order in which the information is presented?

▶ *Layout and design:* What do you notice about the design of the leaflets? You could consider how the writers have used:

- pictures
- different types and sizes of font
- colours and contrast
- length of paragraphs
- how writing is placed in relation to pictures.

2 Re-read the text of the *Volunteering for Oxfam* leaflet closely and make a list of any words the writer has used to suggest to the reader that giving time to Oxfam will be:

a) fun

b) exciting

c) life-changing

d) a way of improving career chances.

3 Look back at the words you listed in question 2. What more do these words suggest about the kind of people whom the writer is trying to persuade?

4 The leaflets use a range of persuasive techniques. Read the following statements and in each case analyse how the writer is persuading the audience to respond. How do these statements make the reader feel? The first one is done for you.

Example

   a) *This week alone I have helped to pay for enough seeds for a family in Malawi to grow a year's supply of food.*

   This statement makes the reader feel that something very valuable has been done very quickly and easily. It encourages the reader to feel he or she can achieve something for others. It could appeal to someone who hasn't got much time.

   b) So take a closer look and surprise yourself.

   c) It will renew your confidence, refresh your skills and provide valuable work experience.

   d) Yes, I want to make a regular gift to Oxfam.

   e) Dirty water led to malaria, swelling of legs and limbs, skin diseases and allergies. Cholera and diarrhoea killed our children.

   f) It's simple to help.

5 a) Now you have read the leaflets in more detail, draw up a chart comparing them on the following points:

   - purpose

   - target audience

   - reasons quotations are included

   - layout and choice of pictures

   - amount and type of information included

   - length of sentences and paragraphs used

   - how simple it is for the reader to do something as a result of reading the leaflet.

   b) Which leaflet do you consider to be more effective in persuading readers to make a commitment to Oxfam? Explain your judgement using evidence from your chart.

W Word level

Identifying verb tenses and modal verbs

1 Both these leaflets try to persuade readers that what they do now can make a difference in the future. To do this they describe how terrible things have been in the **past**; they explain what the situation is like **now**; they suggest how the **future** can be different. Copy and complete the following table by finding examples from the leaflets of sentences written in the **past tense**, in the **present tense** and in the **future tense**. In each case, underline the verb which signals the tense in which the sentence is written.

Past	Present	Future

2 Why do you think the writers move so frequently between tenses in these leaflets?

Modal verbs, such as 'will', 'can', 'would' or 'could', affect the impact of the main verbs which follow them. Here 'can' expresses the possibility of making a difference by donating £2.

Example

*Just £2 from you **can** make a difference.*

3 Look at the paragraph headed 'Money talks' in the *Volunteering for Oxfam* leaflet.

a) Pick out examples where modal verbs are used to alter the impact of main verbs. How does this affect the tone of this persuasive paragraph?

b) Explain whether the use of 'can' would make you more or less likely to get involved.

4 a) Which leaflet includes more examples of the modal verbs 'will' and 'can'?

b) Which leaflet includes more examples of the modal verbs 'could' and 'would'?

c) Briefly explain why you think these modal verbs have been used in each leaflet.

Using language to persuade

Look again at the *Make a gift for life* leaflet. This leaflet depends for impact on convincing readers that:

- they can make things different by giving money
- a simple action from them can help to solve complex problems.

To achieve this, the writer:

- moves between past, present and future to emphasise the difference readers can make
- contrasts complex descriptions of problems in the past with simple instructions on how to change things.

1 Re-read carefully the second page of the leaflet about water, headed 'Just £2 from you can make the difference.'

   a) Identify the tense in which each of the six quotations is written.

   b) How does the use of tense in the quotations correspond to the division of the page into dark and light? What point do you think the writer of the leaflet is trying to make?

2 Compare the following quotations used in the leaflet with the comments from the writer.

- 'Dirty water led to malaria, swelling of legs and limbs, skin diseases and allergies. Cholera and diarrhoea killed our children.' (Garinge Somulu)

- 'It's amazing what just £2 a month from you can do.' (Oxfam leaflet)

▶ 'To get water, we'd leave at midnight one night, and not return until midnight the next day. The water would last two days and then we'd have to go again.' (Howa Fudull)

▶ 'It's simple to help.' (Oxfam leaflet)

   a) What do you notice about the length and complexity of these sentences?

   b) What impact do the quotations have on the reader?

   c) How do the comments from the writer influence the reader?

Discussing and defending your point of view

Although Oxfam does fund charitable work in the UK, these leaflets focus on the help given to people overseas. Some people prefer to see the money they give to charity spent helping people in this country. Other people argue that it is the responsibility of people in richer countries, such as Great Britain, to help those in need in poorer nations.

Think about the following statements expressing different points of view:

- 'We live in a global village and what we do affects the wider world. Our responsibilities are worldwide; if we ignore them, we will all eventually suffer the consequences.'

- 'It's hard to send money overseas when there are people begging on the High Street and children in Britain without homes.'

- 'It's impossible to know if my money will reach the people who need it.'

- 'We know there's enough food and water in the world to sustain everyone. For everyone's sake, our top priority should be to share it more fairly.'

- 'Some charities are huge – I think my money will go into administration, not digging wells.'

- 'Television pictures of innocent people suffering after floods, droughts and earthquakes really upset me. At least giving to charity means I can do something.'

You are going to take part in a class debate on the motion 'This House believes that charity should begin at home.' In groups, discuss whether you want to support or oppose this statement. Some of the views above may help you to decide.

Prepare a short presentation, outlining your group's views and supporting them with any evidence you can find. Try to speak from notes and bullet points rather than a fully written speech. As you stage the debate, consider the views carefully before casting your final vote.

Writing to persuade

 **W** Writing: minor task

You have been asked to present a Christmas charity appeal, encouraging people to donate money to local charities, on a local news programme. Using information from your debate and the leaflets you have read, write a short bulletin, suitable for a one-minute slot on the local news.

Remember – you need to be clear, brief and persuasive. Choose your words carefully. When you have completed the first draft of your bulletin, experiment with reading it out loud. How many words do you need to fill a minute? Keep redrafting until you get it right.

 **W** Writing: major task

In this unit you have been exploring some of the complicated issues surrounding overseas aid. You have been asked to write the text for a leaflet persuading people to give money to charities that help people in other countries, such as victims of earthquakes or famines.

Before you begin to write you need to consider:

- How do you want your audience to feel as they have read the leaflet? Sympathy for people less fortunate than themselves? Angry about the terrible tragedies that occur around the world?

- Who is your audience? Is your leaflet aimed at younger or older readers? Think about how this will affect your decisions about what to include, which words to use and the order in which you present material.

- In what form are you going to present your information? You could include interviews and quotations with charity workers and the people they help.

- When you have gathered your ideas, you need to think about how you are going to organise the text. Make sure you allow enough room to include the most important persuasive points. What headings will you use? You need to make people want to read the leaflet, so you will have to break up a complicated subject into accessible sections.

Use the writing frame on the next page to help you to structure your leaflet.

Headline:

First section

- Engage the reader with a surprising idea.
- Keep the language simple and the heading short and snappy.

Out of sight, out of mind

Did you know that around the world …

Yet just by giving …

Second section

- List reasons for giving overseas aid.
- Explain the positive benefits the aid brings.

Millions of people in poorer countries need …

You may take clean water for granted, but …

Charities working with people in these countries help to …

Third section

- You could include quotations from charities who work overseas.
- Include frequently asked questions and answers about donating to overseas charities.

"By working for Oxfam, I have been able to …"

"Now the charity has helped us to …"

Will all my money go to …

All donations are sent directly to those …

Fourth section

- Encourage the reader to donate to overseas charities in the future.

Remember by giving your money you are helping to …

Help box

1. Try to keep your points clear and brief.
2. Think about using short paragraphs and a variety of simple and complex sentences.
3. Include powerful vocabulary that will encourage your reader to respond.

Unit 8: Argue

Can you prove who you are? Would you want to have to carry a card stating your identity? You are going to look at the arguments for and against identity cards. Firstly, you are going to explore the background to the debate about the use of an identity card system for people in the UK. You are then going to read articles by two journalists who **argue** forcefully about ID cards from different points of view.

Effective writers can be very convincing – but it's important for you to make up your own mind. You need to be able to distinguish facts from opinions and to understand how language can be used to influence what you think. People will always want you to agree with them. You need to develop the skills to sort opinions out for yourself.

Pre-reading

Sometimes it is important to be able to prove your age and identity. Teenagers often use proof of age cards which show the cardholder's name, age and photograph.

1 a) Do you have a proof of age card or any other form of identity card? If you do, when do you use it?

b) Do you think all teenagers should have to carry proof of age cards? What could be the advantages and disadvantages of this?

Older people in Britain can use their passports or driving licences if they need to prove their identity. However, the Government has recently discussed introducing a national identity card (ID card) for everybody over eighteen years of age.

2 Can you think of any advantages to using identity cards? Discuss your ideas with a partner and make a list of the possible advantages.

> Example

> *People who are in favour of a national identity card scheme argue that it would help to cut down on fraud, where criminals steal other people's personal details and use these fake identities to claim benefits that they are not entitled to. Other people think that ID cards could help the fight against terrorism; making it easier to check information about people who are about to travel.*

3 Can you think of any problems that ID cards could bring? Discuss your ideas with a partner and make a list of the possible disadvantages.

> Example

> *People who are against the idea of introducing identity cards argue that it would reduce people's privacy; allowing the people in charge of the scheme to gather information about individuals and use it to spy on them. Other reasons given against using ID cards are the worries about what would happen to the people who didn't carry their identity cards.*

4 In your class, hold a vote to find out whether people are in favour or against the idea of introducing identity cards. When you have read and discussed the two articles about ID cards, vote again to see if anyone's view has been changed by the arguments.

This article is taken from The Guardian, *a broadsheet newspaper, and is written by John O'Farrell, a humorous writer whose articles often take a comical look at serious topical issues. In this article, he puts forward his arguments against introducing ID cards in this country, using a mixture of funny and serious points.*

First, have an identity

By John O'Farrell

It still seems possible that compulsory identity cards will be the response to the heightened state of world tension because the great thing about ID cards is, of course, that they will prevent terrorism. Yup, after years of plotting, encrypted messages, international coordination, secret training and smuggling weapons, the terrorists will be asked for their ID cards and they'll go: "Drat! Foiled at the last minute! All those years of planning and I forgot to forge an identity card!"

ID cards would, of course, represent an outrageous infringement of basic human rights. Because they'd mean regularly presenting strangers with a deeply embarrassing photo of yourself. And to make sure the authorities recognised you from the picture, you'd feel the need to pull the same gawky expression that was momentarily caught in the photo booth at the back of Woolworths.

Whether it means the end of historic freedoms I somehow doubt, but I'm against them for other reasons. They've got all the information they want about us already; the trouble is that most of it is wrong. There is a computer database somewhere that thinks that I, Joan O'Barrell, might be interested in subscribing to the Reader's Digest prize draw. Because the real oppression of identity cards will be the tyranny of having to endure yet another piece of technology that doesn't work properly.

Imagine what fun students will have by drawing an extra couple of lines on each other's bar codes. "I'm afraid, young man, you are not entitled to a student discount because according to the scanner you are a Müller twin-pot yoghurt."

"No, I am a student, really – ask my friend here."

"Well, there's no point in talking to him, he's a small tin of Pokémon pasta shapes."

Those in favour of ID cards talk in glowing terms about the wonders of modern technology. All the information that can possibly be needed about you could be stored on one handy smartcard, replacing all the others in your wallet. A quick swipe will establish that you are prepared to donate your kidneys in the event of an accident, that you are due a free cappuccino at Caffe Nero and that 11 months ago you paid a lot of money to join the local gym but have been only twice. But then police officers will be able to swipe the cards through machines and say: "Look sarge, we've got him now. It says here that 'Barney's Big Adventure' was due back at Blockbuster Video yesterday before 11pm."

"Oh yeah – and look at this: 2,000 Sainsbury reward points accumulated. Been doing a lot of shopping recently haven't we, sonny?"

Because there is, of course, a civil liberties issue. As a middle-class white male I don't suffer much aggravation from the police. Whenever my car is pulled over, I utter a few words and they are suddenly very polite.

But for young black men, failure to produce an identity card on demand could be used as a reason for further harrassment. Asylum seekers, stigmatised enough already, will be made to feel even more like non-persons without an official ID card.

© John O' Farrell
From *The Guardian*

Dictionary check

infringement to go against
gawky stupid
oppression injustice
tyranny cruelty
'Barney's Big Adventure' a children's video

The writer of the next article, Kaizer Nyatsumba, looks at the issue of identity cards through his own personal experiences. Kaizer Nyatsumba is a black South African who lived in South Africa under apartheid. The system of apartheid was a way of keeping people of different races apart and in South Africa at this time black people had fewer freedoms and rights than white people, with restrictions on the jobs that they could do and the places they could go.

There is no need to panic about identity cards

BY KAIZER NYATSUMBA

Some years ago if you were in the US, travelling around the country was quite easy. All you had to produce at airports was a ticket bearing your name, although it might as well have been somebody else's, because no form of identification was required to authenticate ownership of the ticket.

All that changed drastically after 11 September.

For understandable reasons, airports have become a security zone and all passengers are required to show some form of identification with a picture of themselves when checking in and before being allowed to board a plane. The two forms of identification used by most Americans at airports have been their driving licence and their passport. Foreigners like myself could also use both forms of identification, and I never once had a problem using my driving licence for this purpose.

And yet, faced with calls that identity documents may have to be introduced for all, most Americans have been up in arms. They cherish their freedom too much, they say, to want to see it curtailed by having to carry identity documents.

Britain, then, is not alone in its discomfort with identity documents. After all, these tend to be seen as a form of social control that would make it easy for governments to monitor people's movements and perhaps even curtail their much-cherished freedoms.

However, there is nothing about IDs that makes them inherently a bad thing, especially in countries that protect individuals' rights.

As a black South African whose every movement was strictly regulated by the apartheid state in the form of an ID-type document, called a pass book, I ought to be instinctively opposed to the idea of IDs. I am not, however, because there is a big difference between what we have now in South Africa and what we blacks once had to carry on our persons at all times.

As a document that enables one to identify oneself when entering into official or important transactions, an ID, carrying as it does a picture of the owner, is, in my view, a good idea. Not only can it significantly reduce the risk of fraud as a result of impersonation by thieves (unless the ID itself were stolen and the picture changed), but it can also be an aid to the police in the fight against crime.

The demeaning pass books, which required numerous stamps and signatures giving Africans permission to *pass* from one area to another in the country of their birth, were a form of control and had to be carried at all times. Identity documents are an official form of identification and not of control, and hence do not have to be carried along at all times and cannot be demanded by the police. If a crime has been committed, however, the police have the power to drive suspects to their homes so that they can get their IDs to verify that they are indeed who they claim to be.

There is nothing intrinsically wrong or threatening about identity documents, then. It all depends on what they are used for.

Kaizer Nyatsumba
4th July 2002
From *The Independent*

Dictionary check

authenticate prove
cherish love
curtailed reduced

inherently essentially
regulated controlled

demeaning humiliating
intrinsically essentially

Comparing arguments

1 Skim-read the two texts. In each case, identify:

- the context – where was this text published?
- the purpose – what impact does the writer want to have on the readers?
- the audience – who is the writer aiming at?

2 **a)** Make a list of the key points for and against an identity card scheme made in John O'Farrell's article. Do the same for Kaizer Nyatsumba's article.

  b) Compare your two lists. What do you notice about the number of points 'for' and 'against' in each case? Do any points appear in both texts?

  c) Briefly explain what this comparison shows you about the effectiveness of these two articles.

3 Look again at the article 'First, have an identity' by John O'Farrell.

  a) Pick out the quotations John O'Farrell uses in his article. Do they come from real individuals?

  b) What reactions might these quotations provoke in the reader?

  c) Why do you think John O'Farrell has chosen to use this technique? Think about purpose and audience.

4 Look again at the article 'There is no need to panic about identity cards' by Kaizer Nyatsumba.

  a) How often does the writer seem to draw on personal knowledge and experience in this article?

  b) How might this influence the readers' response to his article?

5 **a)** Which newspaper article do you most agree with?

  b) Which newspaper article do you find most memorable and entertaining?

  c) Explain your choices. Try to distinguish between the information the writers chose to use in their arguments – and the skill with which they presented their ideas to you.

W Word level

Using connectives to develop an argument

A writer has to signal clearly to readers how information is linked in order to construct a forceful argument. Writers often use **connectives** – words or phrases which help readers to make the step from one point to the next. Look at Kaizer Nyatsumba's article. At the beginning of each new paragraph he uses a word or phrase which helps the reader to make the link with previous information.

Example

All that changed drastically after 11 September.

This links the relaxed attitude to identity cards in the USA before 11 September 2001, described in paragraph 1, with the drastic changes mentioned in paragraph 3.

1 Copy and complete the following chart to show the opening phrase of each new paragraph in Kaizer Nyatsumba's article. In each case, explain how the phrase makes the link with the previous paragraph. The first one is done for you.

Opening phrase	Explanation
'For understandable reasons'	*This phrase links the events of 11 September, mentioned in paragraph 2, with the developments in security described in paragraph 3.*
'And yet'	*This links the new policy of tighter security mentioned in paragraph 3 with ...*

2 a) Skim-read the article and identify as many connective words and phrases as you can. Here are some to start you off:

- of course
- because
- perhaps.

b) Use as many of these connectives as possible (and others if you wish) to construct a coherent argument explaining to your teacher why you have not been able to hand in your homework today.

Organising your argument

Paragraphs are the building blocks writers use to construct an argument. Writers use them to:

- organise information and focus readers' attention on a particular point

- signal to the reader that the writer is moving on to a new point or idea.

1 a) Draw a flow chart showing the organisation of the article with a box for each paragraph. Write one sentence to summarise the point Kaizer Nyatsumba is making in each box and link them with arrows.

Before 11 September, airport security in the USA was weak.

b) Review your flow chart. Does Kaizer Nyatsumba's argument still work without his persuasive words and phrases?

John O'Farrell's article includes some examples of **colloquial** English, that is words and phrases you would expect to use in conversation rather than see written down in a newspaper. As you complete the following questions, think about the different impact on readers of standard and colloquial English. Do you take one more seriously than the other?

2 a) John O'Farrell uses colloquial language, such as 'yup' and 'drat', in his article. Pick out any other examples that you can find.

b) Do you find his argument more or less persuasive as a result of his colloquial language?

3 Look at the last paragraph of his article. Why do you think he used only standard English here?

Hot seating

Your views on identity cards will be influenced by the impact that having an ID card may have on your life. Different groups of people in society may hold different views to your own. You are going to work in a group of three.

Discuss how having an identity card may affect the following groups of people:

- teenagers (under 18)

- ex-prisoners, seeking work and new lives

- elderly people, entitled to pensions.

Make notes during the discussion to help you with the next part of the activity.

> How we speak has an effect on how we are listened to. The way you talk when you are with your friends is probably different from the language you use when talking to a teacher. You may hardly notice yourself shifting between levels. These different levels of language, adjusted for our audience, are called **registers**. You will need to think about your use of standard and colloquial English in the next part of the activity.

Now each member of the group will play a representative of each of the groups discussed earlier. Use the 'hot seat' technique to question them on their views about identity cards. It is important that each member of the group responds in role to the questions asked.

When the 'hot seat' interviews are over, think about the kind of language each member of the group used. Were they using mainly standard or colloquial English? What impact did this have on the way you listened to their ideas?

Writing to argue

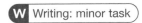 Writing: minor task

Re-read the answer you gave to queston 1 about proof of age cards in the Pre-reading activity. You have been asked to write a short press release which will encourage teenagers to use proof of age cards.

Before you begin to write your press release you will need to consider:

- content – which information is likely to be most relevant and interesting to teenagers?

- language – can you make the tone and register of the language appealing and accessible to teenagers?

- layout – think about your use of paragraphs, questions and answers and bullet points.

 Writing: major task

You are going to write a formal essay presenting the case for and against the introduction of national identity cards. Before you begin to write your essay you need to plan carefully.

First, you should gather your information. Review your lists of advantages and disadvantages of identity cards from the Pre-reading activity. Can you add to these lists? Use this information as the basis for your essay.

Then you need to organise your information. Cut up your lists into individual points. Move these around, regrouping them until they are organised into an order which makes sense to you. The most powerful way to argue is to put the points you disagree with first and then counter them with your own point of view.

When you are happy with the structure you have planned, use the writing frame on the next page to help you to draft the essay.

Introduction

- Hook your audience into reading with a startling or surprising opening statement.
- Explain briefly why identity cards are an issue for discussion.

The case against

- Begin with the side of the argument that you don't agree with.
- Use a paragraph for each point you want to make.
- Use connectives such as 'of course' and 'furthermore' to link your points together.

The case for

- Now put the points you agree with.
- Again, use a paragraph for each point.
- Connectives such as 'but', 'and yet', 'however' and 'although' will help you.
- Try to use these points to undermine the other side of the case by making links.

Conclusion

- Review very briefly the case for and against.
- Conclude with your own opinion.
- Try to express this in an appealing and memorable way, so it stays with the reader.

Help box

1 Think about your use of standard English.

Unit 9: Advise

Where do you go for **advice**? You are going to read three web pages from Channel 4's youth website 'T4'. The first two deal with specific questions from readers; the third offers a ten-point advice plan on how to avoid stress at work. Writers offering advice have to be both very aware of the impact their writing may have on readers and also sensitive to readers' needs. No one wants to be told what to do – so writing to advise can also mean writing to reassure, to inform and to offer choices. Before you read, make a list of places you could go for advice on the following issues: school problems; relationships; worries at home; issues that worry you in the wider world. Where do you think your parents could have gone for advice when they were your age? What changes have there been in where people go for advice?

Just ask: Rachel's question

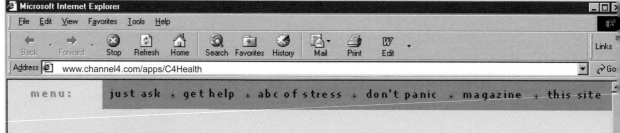

Microsoft Internet Explorer

File   Edit   View   Favorites   Tools   Help

Back   Forward   Stop   Refresh   Home   Search   Favorites   History   Mail   Print   Edit   Links

Address   www.channel4.com/apps/C4Health   Go

menu: just ask + get help + abc of stress + don't panic + magazine + this site

just ask

Rachel, a 13-year-old female, asked the following question on Thu 02/Aug/01 09:01 pm

Question

Sometimes, I can't sleep and get bugged by my thoughts. It may be stupid things from ages ago but, sometimes, things quite big (for instance, I need a new sim card AND my PUK code for my phone. I don't know how to approach the network company to ask them.)

It creeps me out and, whatever time it may be, it makes me feel really bad. I haven't told anyone yet. Should I?

Answer

You sound quite anxious about not being able to sleep. Many problems with sleep are because you're worried about something. Sometimes you're worried but you've blocked it out during the day. At night, it comes back and nags at you. Then you worry about not sleeping. This can go on for days.

It might be useful to speak to an older person that you trust, perhaps a member of your family, or a teacher. They may be able to put your mind at ease. If you are not feeling confident about contacting the phone network, maybe someone else can help you. There is nothing wrong with asking for help.

If you want to speak to someone who doesn't know you, you could contact ChildLine on 0800 1111, anytime, day or night. You would be able to speak to an advisor about your bad feelings and it would be completely confidential.

ChildLine also has a website:

www.childline.org.uk/welcome/kids.htm

The website below may also be useful for you:

www.lifebytes.gov.uk/mental/mental_stress.html

I hope this is helpful.

Done   Internet

Just ask: Natalie's question

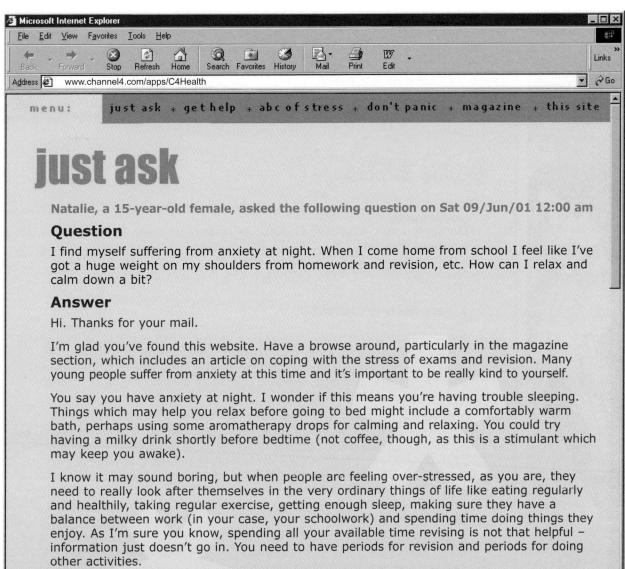

Microsoft Internet Explorer

File Edit View Favorites Tools Help

Back · Forward · Stop Refresh Home Search Favorites History Mail Print Edit   Links »

Address www.channel4.com/apps/C4Health   Go

menu: just ask + get help + abc of stress + don't panic + magazine + this site

just ask

Natalie, a 15-year-old female, asked the following question on Sat 09/Jun/01 12:00 am

Question

I find myself suffering from anxiety at night. When I come home from school I feel like I've got a huge weight on my shoulders from homework and revision, etc. How can I relax and calm down a bit?

Answer

Hi. Thanks for your mail.

I'm glad you've found this website. Have a browse around, particularly in the magazine section, which includes an article on coping with the stress of exams and revision. Many young people suffer from anxiety at this time and it's important to be really kind to yourself.

You say you have anxiety at night. I wonder if this means you're having trouble sleeping. Things which may help you relax before going to bed might include a comfortably warm bath, perhaps using some aromatherapy drops for calming and relaxing. You could try having a milky drink shortly before bedtime (not coffee, though, as this is a stimulant which may keep you awake).

I know it may sound boring, but when people are feeling over-stressed, as you are, they need to really look after themselves in the very ordinary things of life like eating regularly and healthily, taking regular exercise, getting enough sleep, making sure they have a balance between work (in your case, your schoolwork) and spending time doing things they enjoy. As I'm sure you know, spending all your available time revising is not that helpful – information just doesn't go in. You need to have periods for revision and periods for doing other activities.

Activities you may like to try which may help you relax would include yoga, going for a walk or a swim, going to the gym, or dancing, making sure that you get to see your friends and spend at least some part of each day doing something for your own enjoyment. Also I wonder if you have someone to confide in about how you are feeling? Just knowing that someone else knows and cares about what you're going through can help. I wonder how easy it is for you to confide in someone in your family, for instance?

You might find it helpful to talk through how you're feeling with a stranger, in which case you could try calling Youth2Youth, a national helpline for young people, run by young people. Their phone number is 020 8896 3675. Another possibility would be ChildLine, who deal with many calls from young people on the subject of exam stress. Their number is 0800 1111.

It can also sometimes help to keep a diary – writing out your thoughts and feelings can help you to express exactly what is going on for you.

Good luck, I hope all goes well for you.

Done   Internet

Don't panic

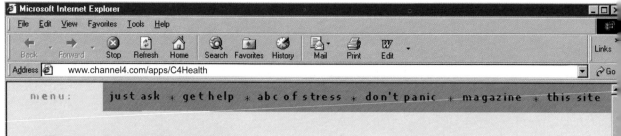

File   Edit   View   Favorites   Tools   Help

Back   Forward   Stop   Refresh   Home   Search   Favorites   History   Mail   Print   Edit   Links

Address   www.channel4.com/apps/C4Health   Go

menu: just ask + get help + abc of stress + don't panic + magazine + this site

don't panic

Stressbusters

Losing your cool? Can't cope? Feeling stressed? Here are 10 common-sense tips which can help you beat that stress. Remember, they are not the Ten Commandments. Giving yourself more rules – on top of life's existing demands – will only make matters worse. Just pick the ideas you find helpful.

1 Stop beating yourself up

You don't need to be perfect. It is OK to do work that is good enough. Perfectionists are often the first victims of stress. You don't have to excel all the time. When you take on a task, check what is expected. There is no point in writing a 24-page report when all that is needed is a brief memo. And we all make mistakes. If you give a dud presentation, write it off to experience. It does not mean you personally are a failure.

2 Stop saying yes

Don't take on more than you can handle. Be assertive. It is OK to say no to other people's demands. You just need the right technique. Try saying: 'Yes, I can do this report but that will mean I cannot make that meeting.' Or simply say: 'Thank you for asking me but I am afraid I would not be able to meet that deadline.' Let people know how busy you are. You can put a red card on your computer when you don't want to be interrupted, a green one when that's OK.

3 Stop and think

Stand back, take a few minutes to weigh up your workload and plan your day. Make sure that you don't let emergencies – like the crisis in accounts – overtake those that are more important but less immediately pressing – such as planning next year's spending. Delegate jobs where you can.

4 Stop and talk

Express yourself. It is good to talk. Communicating with other people – colleagues, friends and family – is a great way to beat stress, whether you are pouring out your worries or just passing the time of day. Talk to your boss or line manager too or, if appropriate, to anyone else at work who might be able to help, such as the human resources team. When you have a particular problem don't be afraid to seek help from others. If colleagues, friends or family can't help, try helplines where they exist.

5 Stop rushing

We all have different ways of working. Some people love to live life in the fast lane. But most of us cannot work at breakneck pace every hour of the day. If we do, our performance suffers. Build in time to unwind and reflect.

6 Stop for lunch

Take a break. Making sure you have lunch, or a mealbreak during your shift, means you get a vital rest from work demands, a chance to socialise with colleagues or friends, and ensures you eat properly too. You should aim to have a balanced lunch and try to avoid alcohol, smoking and caffeine if possible. Not eating properly – snacking on crisps and chocolate bars or binge eating at the end of the day – is a sure sign of stress and may make you ill. It is also a legal requirement that you get a meal break during your day.

7 Stop and take a walk

Exercise your stress away. The adrenaline we build up under stress needs a release. Sport and exercise – whether walking, cycling, swimming or whatever else turns you on – is one of the greatest stressbusters. It gives your mind and body a positive challenge. It is virtually impossible to think negatively while pedalling. Try it!

8 Stop and breathe

Taking a few minutes out to relax during a busy day is important. Breathing properly is a great way to do it. You can practise deep-breathing exercises from yoga or meditation. Or try this simple exercise. Sit quietly at your desk, shut your eyes and try to concentrate. Let stressful thoughts float away. Breathe in for three seconds, then out for nine. Repeat for a minute or two.

9 Stop working late

Staying healthy means keeping life in balance. Working long hours – whether that means staying late in the office or putting in extra time on shifts – is bad for your health, your performance and your family. We all need time to unwind, to be with family and friends, to have space for ourselves and to enjoy hobbies or sports that have nothing to do with work. Work smarter, not longer.

10 Stop taking work home

It is easy to feel under pressure to take work home, just because everyone else does. The culture expects it. Break the mould. We all need boundaries between work and the rest of life to keep sane. Smarter organisations are now discouraging staff from working beyond reasonable limits. Remember the motto: 'Work to live, not live to work'.

Get help

Need more help? If you feel under excessive stress or are suffering any physical effects from stress you should see your GP or seek help elsewhere. There are numerous organisations which can help you tackle stress in our 'get help' directory, which is compiled with the help of stress management consultant Roger Mead.

If you have your own stressbusters we'd love to hear about them and why they work. They may even get on the site! E-mail us at stress@channel4.com

T Text level: reading

Internet advice

1 Skim-read these web pages. Think about the following features:

- the menu and options offered
- the headings for each web page
- details given in the two 'letters' about the people asking for advice
- use of numbering and subheadings in the 'Don't panic' web page
- details of links to other websites.

2 a) Which characteristics of these web pages seem to you to be most effective and helpful?

    b) Are there any layout and format features that you didn't find helpful?

3 Some issues on these pages are very personal. What are the advantages and disadvantages of using websites as places to discuss personal problems and to get individual advice?

4 Compare the two 'Just ask' web pages with the 'Don't panic' web page.

    a) List any clues you can find about the intended audiences for these pages. Look at the language used as well as the subject matter.

    b) Write a sentence describing the intended audience for the 'Just ask' web pages and another for the 'Don't panic' web page based on the evidence you have found.

5 Look at the following advice from the three texts.

- 'It might be helpful to speak to an older person' ('Just ask: Rachel's question')
- 'You might find it helpful to talk through how you are feeling' ('Just ask: Natalie's question')
- 'Be assertive' ('Don't panic')
- 'You could contact Childline' ('Just ask: Rachel's question')
- 'It can also sometimes help to keep a diary' ('Just ask: Natalie's question')
- 'Stop rushing' ('Don't panic')

a) The 'Just ask' advice includes **modal verbs** such as 'can', 'might' and 'could'. What effect do these have?

b) The 'Don't panic' text uses the imperative form of verbs like 'Be' and 'Stop'. How does the use of the imperative form affect the impact of the advice given?

c) What is the effect on the reader of repeating 'Stop' in the sub-headings of the 'Don't panic' text?

6 Compare the different way advice is offered in the 'Just ask' texts with the 'Don't panic' text. What does this suggest about the different purposes of the texts?

> The writers of all three texts use a range of techniques to reassure readers and offer them options to choose from in addressing problems.

7 Continue the list below, identifying as many techniques as you can.

- reassuring the reader that he or she is not unusual
- offering practical information and contacts
- boosting the reader's self-confidence
- offering suggestions.

8 Choose one piece of advice offered in these texts which you think will be helpful and one which you think won't work. In each case, describe the example you have chosen and explain why you think this piece of advice will or will not be effective.

Unit 9: Advise

W Word level

Doubling consonants

When writing under the pressure of time in tests you can sometimes make spelling mistakes. To help you to avoid making errors in your key stage 3 test you are going to review your understanding of the spelling rules which tell you when to **double consonants**.

Remember:

- A consonant is any letter which isn't a vowel ('a','e', 'i', 'o', 'u').
- A double consonant affects the sound of the vowel before it. Compare the sounds of the following:

Example

'later' with 'latter'

'writer' with 'written'

'taping' with 'tapped'

A long vowel becomes short when followed by a double consonant.

If you add 'ed' or 'ing' to a verb which ends in a single consonant, you usually have to double the consonant to keep the vowel sound the same.

Example

let + ing = letting

tip + ed = tipped

1 a) Look at the following groups of words. For each group decide whether or not you would double consonants.

Group one	Group two	Group three
pedal	*express*	*help*
plug	*pass*	*expect*
fit	*drill*	*work*
slap	*roll*	*talk*

b) In which group or groups did you double consonants? Explain why.

Formal and colloquial language

Asking for advice can be scary – so writers have to make the right impact and help readers to feel welcomed and safe. Writers of advice need to consider:

- **register** – how formal or informal to sound

- **vocabulary** – how to choose words which will make the reader feel comfortable

- **structure** – how simple or complicated to make sentences and paragraphs.

Working together, these elements can help the writer to establish a welcoming tone.

1 Re-read the opening paragraphs of the answers in the 'Just ask' web pages and the opening paragraph of the 'Don't panic' web page.

   a) Why does the writer of the answer to Rachel's question use 'you' and 'you're' so often in this first paragraph?

   b) Comment on the impact of 'Hi. Thanks for your mail,' in the advice given to Natalie. How might this make the reader feel?

   c) Why does the writer of the 'Don't panic' text begin with several questions?

2 Skim-read these web pages again and compile a resource bank of words and phrases which the writers use to offer reassurance to their readers.

Example

Trust, helpful, speak to someone, unwind, enjoyment, I'm sure you know ...

In the 'Just ask' web pages both the questions and the answers seem almost as if the readers and writers are speaking to each other. This is because the writer uses **colloquial language**. This includes vocabulary which might normally be spoken rather than written, such as 'dud', 'cool', 'binge' and which may not be used grammatically.

3 Imagine you are a doctor, recording symptoms of stress for your patients' records. Rewrite the following colloquial phrases from the 'Just ask' web pages in formal English.

a) Sometimes, I can't sleep and get bugged by my thoughts.

Doctor's notes

The patient complained that ...

b) It creeps me out and, whatever time it may be, it makes me feel really bad.

c) I feel like I've got a huge weight on my shoulders from homework, revision, etc.

4 a) Pick out three pieces of advice from the 'Don't panic' web page which are expressed in colloquial English.

b) Rewrite these pieces of advice for a medical textbook, suggesting practical advice which could be given to patients suffering from stress. You need to use clear and formal language.

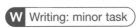

Problem solving

In this activity you are going to develop your listening skills and also think about the best ways to give advice.

First, write down on a piece of paper a problem which might be an issue for people of your age such as exam stress. Don't make the problem personal or embarrassing. You should then post this problem into a box which is kept by your teacher.

You are now going to work in a group of three. Your teacher will give you three problems to discuss from the box. In your group you should discuss one problem at a time. During your discussion think carefully about the following questions:

- What does this writer need?
- How can we reassure her or him?
- What options can we offer?

When you have worked on all three problems, choose the one you feel you have dealt with most effectively to share with the rest of the class. When you have shared your response, ask the rest of the class to comment how effective your advice is likely to be.

Writing to advise

Look back at the advice given to Natalie on page 99. You are going to write the text captions for three cartoon pictures that show this advice.

First of all, make a list of the advice that Natalie is given and choose the three most important points. Then briefly describe what each cartoon picture would show and write the text caption that would accompany it.

W Writing: major task

You are going to create your own problem for the T4 website and write three answers responding to the issues raised. You could use one of the problems you discussed in the Speaking and listening activity or create a new one.

Use the following writing frame to help you.

The problem

- Decide on the age and gender of the writer and the nature of the problem.
- Choose an issue which will appeal to users of the website.
- Write the problem in an e-mail format.
- Use a register and style which matches the age and gender of the writer.

Response 1

- This advice could be from someone of the same age and gender as the writer. It could be someone who is facing a similar issue.
- Think carefully about the style and register of this response – how will this writer offer reassurance and help?
- Make sure the response addresses the issues in the e-mail.

Response 2

- This advice could be from an expert, such as a teacher, doctor or counsellor.
- Think about the different point of view they would offer on the problem.
- Contrast the style and register with the previous response.

Response 3

- This advice could be from someone of your choice, such as the editor of the website or a parent.
- Match the style and register to the writer.
- Try to give advice that hasn't already been offered in the other two responses.

Help box

1. Try to choose vocabulary which will make the reader feel comfortable and use colloquial language where appropriate.

2. Think about the effects you can create by including modal verbs like 'can', 'might' and 'could'.

Review of revision objectives

W1 Revise spelling conventions

When you are writing in a test you will sometimes make spelling errors because you are under pressure of time. It's important to know before you go into the test what the spelling errors are that you are most likely to make and what the spelling rules are that will help you. Look at this list of some of the most common spelling mistakes pupils made in their key stage 3 tests:

▶ Not being sure when to double consonants. The rule is that when words end in a single consonant preceded by a short vowel, double the consonant before adding -ing, -er, or -est.

> Example
>
> dig ──────▶ digging   beep ──────▶ beeping

▶ Not knowing how to add endings to words that end in an 'e'. The rule is that if the word ends in an 'e' it will usually drop the 'e' if the ending begins with a vowel. If the word ends in 'e' and the ending begins with a consonant, then it will keep its 'e'.

> Example
>
> love ──────▶ loving   take ──────▶ taking
> love ──────▶ lovely   hope ──────▶ hopeful

▶ Not knowing whether when 'full' is added to a word it keeps a double 'l'. The rule is that the second 'l' is dropped.

> Example
>
> beautiful   pitiful   colourful

You are now going to make for yourself a 'check card'. On it you will keep a list of useful spelling information which will help you to look for and identify the kind of mistakes that you might make. You should use your 'check card' to help you check through your work every time you hand in a piece of writing.

> You won't be able to get all of the information you need onto the 'check card', so you will have to select the most important points you need to remember. Write on both sides of the card.

> Include the following:
> - the spelling rules you need to remember
> - the words you most often misspell
> - words you often confuse.

Analyse, review, comment

This section introduces you to three types of writing that you will find very useful now in Year 9 and also as you study for your GCSEs. Writing to analyse, review and comment is when the writer seeks to present a view of a situation, text, issue or set of ideas.

Analysis requires you to explore a situation, text, issue or set of ideas in depth. Writers who produce analytical writing employ the skills of selecting evidence and examples to back up the points that they wish to make and then organising these points in a way that convinces the reader that they understand the issues or ideas analysed.

Writing a **review** is a process close to writing persuasively as well as writing analytically. The purpose of a review is to make clear to the reader the personal opinion of the writer and to persuade the reader that this opinion is the right one. The job of a review writer, like the writer of an analytical piece, is to select evidence to back up their opinion and then to express that opinion in a way that convinces the reader. They have to both analyse and persuade through their writing – a complex job, requiring them to use vocabulary that describes, evaluates and persuades.

The word **'comment'** is one that you will find on almost all examination papers at GCSE because in this form of writing the writer is required to explain their thinking about the issues or ideas with which they are presented. The best commentary analyses in depth an idea, an issue or a text, making points that are organised in sequence. At the same time the writing presents a personal viewpoint or opinion. Commentary therefore joins together the skills of analysis and review.

As you work through the next three units you will see how these different types of writing are closely related, sharing similar features and often using the same techniques.

Unit 10: Analyse

In Year 9 you will be expected to develop your skills in **analysing** texts. This is a skill that you will need in key stage 4 for your GCSE examination papers, in a whole range of subjects. Analysing requires you to consider ideas or issues in depth, to offer your interpretations of them and then to back up your thinking with evidence and examples.

In this unit you are going to look at three pieces of writing from very different sources, which together make up a case study on the subject of TV violence. Each of the texts analyses the subject from a different angle and comes up with a different conclusion. At the end of the unit you will consider which analysis best corresponds to your own views on the issues being considered. Before you read, think about which of the following sources of information you would use if you needed to find out true and accurate information: the Internet; television news; tabloid newspapers; interviews. Explain why you think some sources of information are more reliable than others.

Address www.gnfc.org.uk/tv_violn.html.co

| Home | Articles | News | Research | Advice |

A free resource for parents from
Good News
FAMILY CARE

Please feel free to print one copy of this article.

Children and TV violence

Children in Britain watch an average of three to four hours of television daily. Television can be a powerful influence in developing value systems and shaping behaviour. Unfortunately, much of today's television programming is violent. Hundreds of studies of the effects of violence on television have found that children and teenagers may:

- **become 'immune' to the horror of violence**
- **gradually accept violence as a way to solve problems**
- **imitate the violence they observe on television**
- **identify with certain characters, victims and/or victimisers.**

Extensive viewing of television violence by children causes greater aggressiveness. Sometimes, watching a single violent programme can increase aggressiveness. Children who view shows in which violence is realistic, frequently repeated or unpunished, are more likely to imitate what they see. Children with emotional, behavioural, learning or impulse control problems may be more easily influenced by TV violence. The impact of TV violence may be immediately evident in the child's behaviour or may surface years later, and young people can even be affected when the family atmosphere shows no tendency toward violence.

While TV violence is not the only cause of aggressive or violent behaviour, it is clearly a significant factor.

You can protect your children from excessive TV violence in the following ways:
- pay attention to the programmes your children are watching and watch some with them
- set limits on the amount of time they spend with the television
- consider removing the TV set from the child's bedroom – or making the set 'video only'
- point out that although the actor has not actually been hurt or killed, such violence in real life results in pain or death
- refuse to let children see shows known to be violent, and change the channel or turn off the TV set when offensive material comes on, with an explanation of what is wrong with the programme
- disapprove of the violent episodes in front of the children, stressing the belief that such behaviour is not the best way to resolve a problem
- to offset peer pressure among friends and classmates, contact other parents and agree to enforce similar rules about the length of time and types of programme the children may watch.

You can also adopt these measures to prevent harmful effects from television in other areas such as racial or sexual stereotyping. The amount of time children watch TV, regardless of content, should be moderated because it decreases time spent on more active and creative pastimes such as reading, playing with friends and developing hobbies.

From Good Family News Care

Dictionary check

value systems the beliefs and values people have
impulse control problems the inability to control behaviour

nature

scienceupdate

news

Blow for teens' TV time

Violent behaviour in later life could be linked to teenage viewing habits.

Teenagers who watch more than one hour of television a day are more likely to become violent adults, say US researchers. The large-scale, long-term study is one of the first to show such effects on adolescents and young adults.

Current advice on TV viewing, such as the American Academy of Pediatrics' recommendation of 1–2 hours per day, might set the bar too high, says Jeffrey Johnson of Columbia University in New York, a member of the research team. 'If parents want to minimize the risk that their children grow up to commit aggressive acts, they should attempt to limit their viewing to less than one hour per day, on average,' he says.

Many psychologists regard the link between media violence and violent behaviour as well established. Other researchers see it as unproven, and say that the new study is flawed.

On the box

Johnson and his colleagues have been following 707 families in upstate New York since 1975. They used statistics to separate TV viewing from other factors contributing to aggressive behaviour, such as family income, education and prior history of violence. The team hopes it has split the possibility that television causes aggression from the possibility that aggressive people watch lots of television.

1 to 2 hours TV a day could be too much for teenagers.

The biggest jump in aggressive behaviour occurred between adolescents who watched less than one hour of TV per day and those who watched 1–3 hours, all other things being equal, the researchers found.

The trend towards violence continued with increased viewing. Children who watched three or more hours of TV per day between the ages of 14 and 16 were roughly five times more likely to commit violent acts as adults than those who watched less than one hour.

The new study shows that youths are vulnerable to the effects of media violence over a broad age range, says psychologist Craig Anderson of Iowa State University in Ames. 'We can't sit back and say that after 12 it no longer matters.'

'People may be particularly sensitive to the effects of media violence in early adolescence,' says Johnson. 'It's a critical period of life for the development of social skills and personalities.'

Spoiling the view

But other psychologists criticize the study's methods. The way that Johnson's team divided people by their viewing habits invalidates their results, says Guy Cumberbatch, who heads the Communications Research Group, a UK company that does broadcasting and social-policy research.

Only 88 adolescents averaged less than one hour in front of the box each day, he points out. This group is 'so small, it's aberrant,' he says – its members will probably have many other characteristics not reported in this study, such as being teachers' offspring or devoutly religious.

It would have been better to split children into high, medium and low viewing groups, rather than force them into categories, Cumberbatch believes. Johnson's team has 'tortured the data till they confess,' he goes on, calling the group's conclusions 'a remarkable feat of topsy-turvy logic'. Johnson counters that dividing TV viewers into the groups that Cumberbatch suggests would not have affected the study's basic results.

John Whitfield
From *Nature*, 29 March 2002

Dictionary check

long-term study a study conducted over a long period of time
invalidates makes worthless
aberrant not true to its purpose

TV violence on the increase

Jason Deans

The realistic portrayal of violence in TV drama increased significantly in 1999, according to Broadcasting Standard Commission research.

1999 was the year in which EastEnders fell foul of the BSC for the graphic depiction of Steve Owen's murder of scheming Saskia.

In total, 692 scenes of fictional violence were recorded in 1999 and 68% were regarded as realistic.

This compares with 62% in 1998, according to the BSC.

The number of violent scenes also increased markedly in 1999, up to 1,356 from 1,230 in 1998, according to the BSC.

Much of this increase was put down to coverage of the Kosovo conflict.

News and current affairs accounted for 28% of all depictions of violence on UK terrestrial channels in 1999.

The amount of swearing and bad language on terrestrial TV rose significantly in the 1990s, according to BSC research.

In 1999, the BSC recorded 2,887 incidents of offensive language, the highest since the regulator began its tracking survey in 1993.

In 1993 there were just over 2,000 incidents of bad language.

Only 5% of shows were felt to contain a significant amount of violence and 4% had notable levels of strong language.

From *The Guardian*,
Monday 29 January, 2001

T Text level: reading

Analysing the evidence

Questions 1–3 are about the article 'Children and TV violence'.

1 Scan the text and answer the following questions:

   a) Who wrote this text and who is the intended audience?

   b) Where would you find it and how do you know this?

   c) Why is the text free?

2 Read the text closely. Summarise in three sentences the argument that this article is putting forward.

3 Read the second paragraph of the text beginning 'Extensive viewing …' carefully. Work with a partner to answer the following:

   a) What seven points are being made here about the impact of watching television on young people? Pick out the evidence used to back up these points.

   b) Why does the writer use words and phrases such as 'sometimes', 'can', 'more likely to', 'may be', 'may' and 'can even'? Do you think these words and phrases make the arguments more or less effective?

Questions 4–6 are about the article 'Blow for teens' TV time'.

4 Read the article closely. Using information from the article, explain why John Whitfield says that 'violent behaviour in later life **could be** linked to teenage viewing habits' not that violent behaviour '**is** linked to teenage viewing habits'.

5 In the third paragraph beginning 'Current advice …' Jeffrey Johnson offers advice to parents about their children's viewing. What differences do you notice between the way this advice is expressed compared with the advice given in the third paragraph of the article 'Children and TV violence'?

6 a) Skim the text to find the sentence that introduces the other side of the argument about children and television violence, and write this down.

b) Critics of the survey say that Johnson's team was 'torturing the data' until it confessed. Explain in your own words what this means and work with a partner to find out why the data is being criticised.

Questions 7–9 are about the report 'TV violence on the increase'.

7 Scan the report. What are the two main differences between this text and the other two in the case study?

8 Now read the text closely. Consider the following statements and choose which one best matches your view:

i) The writer of this text wants to persuade the reader that TV violence affects young people.

ii) The writer of this text wants to show TV violence is on the increase.

iii) The writer of this text wants to show that TV violence is on the increase and that this affects young people.

9 a) Briefly explain what is the main reason for the increase in the number of incidents of TV violence.

b) Look back to the text 'Children and TV violence'. According to that text, how much of the violence and offensive language listed here is likely to have an effect on young people?

Ways of checking

You will increasingly encounter words you don't fully understand as you begin to read more widely, so it's important that you don't forget the spelling strategies you have learned earlier in school. Look carefully at the five key spelling strategies listed below:

- Look for a root word and try to work out the meaning from that.

- Read to the end of the sentence, then guess the meaning of the word/phrase in context.

- Use a dictionary.

- Work out the meaning of the words that you recognise and try to build the sense from there.

- Think of other words you know that are similar.

1 Which strategies would you use to work out the meaning of the following words and phrases taken from the case study texts:

a) racial and sexual stereotyping ('Children and TV violence')

b) pediatric ('Blow for teens' TV time')

c) psychologist ('Blow for teens' TV time')

d) terrestial TV ('TV violence on the increase')?

2 After using these strategies provide brief definitions for each of the words or phrases listed above.

S Sentence level

Making ideas clear

Analytical writing requires you to make points simply and clearly, then to write about those points, exploring and explaining them. Most analytical writing is in standard English, because it is important that the reader understands exactly what is being said, and standard English is very clear and precise. Most writers will use complex sentences when writing analysis, because this way they can pack in lots of information into each sentence.

1 Study the following paragraph, taken from 'Children and TV violence'.

Example

Extensive viewing of television violence by children causes greater aggressiveness. Sometimes, watching a single violent programme can increase aggressiveness. Children who view shows in which violence is realistic, frequently repeated or unpunished, are more likely to imitate what they see. Children with emotional, behavioural, learning or impulse control problems may be more easily influenced by TV violence. The impact of the TV violence may be immediately evident in the child's behaviour or may surface years later, and young people can even be affected when the family atmosphere shows no tendency towards violence.

a) The writer makes two points in this paragraph and then analyses these points in detail. Write out the two sentences which contain these points.

b) If you were editing this piece of writing, where could you put in a paragraph break?

c) How does the writer link together the second and third sentence with the first? Quote from the text to support your answer.

2 Look again at the third sentence:

> Example

> *Children who view shows in which violence is realistic, frequently repeated or unpunished, are more likely to imitate what they see.*

    a) Identify the main clause in this sentence.

    b) Rewrite the sentence as two simple sentences, containing the same information. (You should try to keep the same words as far as possible, though you will have to change some words and add in others.)

    c) Look at the two versions. Which is more effective at conveying the information, and why?

3 This article is written for parents. If you were writing the same article for teenagers would you use standard English? Explain the reasons for your answer.

SL Speaking and listening

Analysing problems and solutions

Working in a pair you are going to read and consider the following statements that offer guidance about television watching to help adults who are caring for children.

▶ Pay attention to the programmes your children are watching and watch some with them.

▶ Set limits on the amount of time children spend with the television.

▶ Remove the TV set from the child's bedroom or make the set 'video only'.

▶ Allow children to watch any amount of television – they will only watch it at their friends' houses if you don't.

▶ Refuse to let children see shows known to be violent and change the channel or turn off the TV set when offensive material comes on, then explain what is wrong with the programme.

▶ Do not have a television in your home.

▶ Allow children to watch such programmes, but disapprove of violent episodes in front of the children, stressing the belief that such behaviour is not the best way to resolve a problem.

▶ Contact other parents and agree to enforce similar rules about the length of time and type of programmes children may watch.

With your partner, choose five statements and analyse each of them in turn. Copy and complete the table below to help you to organise and record your discussion.

Statement	Strengths of this idea	Weaknesses of this idea	Other issues that would need to be thought about
Remove the TV set from the child's bedroom or make the set 'video only'			

When you have analysed each of the five statements, prepare a spoken statement for the rest of the class, in which you and your partner present a brief analysis of the issues parents have to consider when deciding how or whether children should watch television.

Writing to analyse

W | Writing: minor task

You are now going to devise a questionnaire to use on your classmates to gather information about their attitudes to violence on television. The focus of your questionnaire is 'Does violence on television affect the way young people behave?' You need to write five questions.

- Ask questions which encourage people to express their views. If you ask questions to which people can reply 'yes' or 'no' you will not have a great deal to work on when you write up your findings.
- Don't ask ambiguous questions – make sure you have expressed the question clearly so that people reading the questionnaire know exactly what they are being asked.

Now work with a partner to decide on the questions you are going to ask. Try to ask questions that will find out:

- what people believe to be true about this issue
- whether they have themselves been affected by TV violence
- whether they think other people that they know or have heard about have been affected by it.

When you have completed the first draft of your questionnaire you should try it out on one or two pupils. Look at the answers that you collect and make any necessary changes to the questions in order to get better answers. Once you are happy with the questionnaire you can use it on five pupils and collect the answers to your questions.

W | Writing: major task

You are now going to analyse the information from your questionnaires and write a 500-word report on the findings. First of all you will need to divide the information you have from your questionnaire into three sections:

- what people believe about the issue – i.e. that children are affected by TV violence or they aren't or that some are and some aren't
- whether they have themselves been affected by TV violence and if that has been harmful or not
- whether they think other people that they know or have heard about have been affected by it.

Use the writing frame below to help you organise your report.

Paragraph one

We carried out a survey of ...

We asked the following questions ...

Our overall findings from the survey show that ...

Paragraph two

We began by trying to find out what pupils believed to be true about the links between television and violence.

Some/most/a few pupils said that ...

A few pupils thought that ...

We found these answers interesting/unexpected/unsurprising because ...

Of most interest to us was the pupil who said that ...

This was particularly fascinating because ...

It didn't surprise us that ...

Paragraph three

Then we went on to explore whether pupils thought they were themselves ever affected by TV violence.

We found some striking examples of pupils being affected, for example ...

Most pupils were/weren't affected ...

Paragraph four

Lastly, we asked pupils if they knew of other people being affected by TV violence.

Most people said that ...

However, a few thought that ...

We noted some interesting examples, such as ...

Particular programmes such as ...

One pupil said that ...

This fits in/doesn't fit in with what pupils said in answer to ...

Paragraph five

Our survey helped us to find out that ...

Before we began the research we thought that ...

Our ideas have been confirmed/partially confirmed/have proved to be wrong because ...

What we found most interesting in this analysis was ...

What we would now like to find out would be ...

Help box

1 Use phrases such as 'sometimes', 'can', 'more likely to', 'may be', 'can even' to link your analysis to your findings.

Unit 11: Review

By now you will be experienced at **reviewing**. You will have written book reviews yourself and be used to reading reviews of television programmes and films before you decide if they are worth watching. In this unit you are going to look at two slightly different forms of review: the first is a review of the first Harry Potter book, *Harry Potter and the Philosopher's Stone*, which was posted on an online bookshop's website and the second is a leaflet produced by a company which is selling a new computer game. You will explore how the writers of these texts use the conventions of a review to fit their purposes in writing. At the end of the unit, you will have the opportunity to create your own leaflet to review and sell a computer game and also write a review suitable for a web page.

Pre-reading

Work with a partner to decide what are the three most important things you would consider before you bought the following:

- a computer game you hadn't ever played before
- a fiction book to read for pleasure.

Write a list placing the factors in order of importance.

Amazon.co.uk review

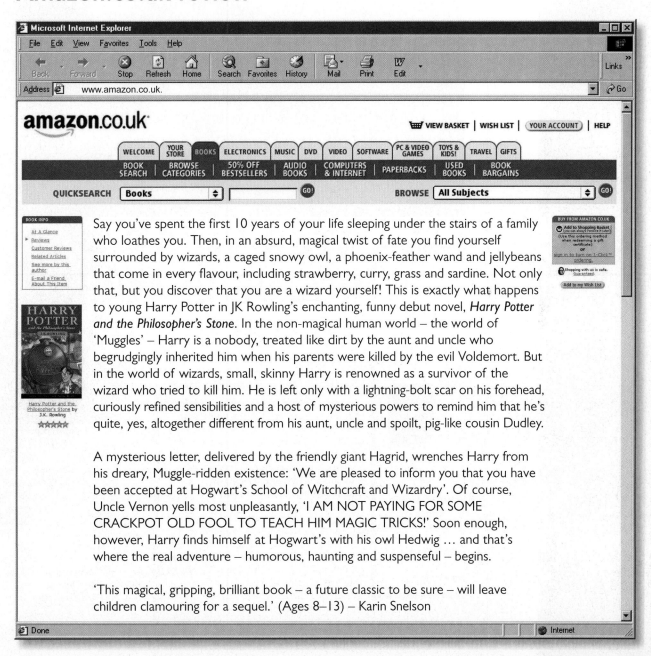

Say you've spent the first 10 years of your life sleeping under the stairs of a family who loathes you. Then, in an absurd, magical twist of fate you find yourself surrounded by wizards, a caged snowy owl, a phoenix-feather wand and jellybeans that come in every flavour, including strawberry, curry, grass and sardine. Not only that, but you discover that you are a wizard yourself! This is exactly what happens to young Harry Potter in JK Rowling's enchanting, funny debut novel, *Harry Potter and the Philosopher's Stone*. In the non-magical human world – the world of 'Muggles' – Harry is a nobody, treated like dirt by the aunt and uncle who begrudgingly inherited him when his parents were killed by the evil Voldemort. But in the world of wizards, small, skinny Harry is renowned as a survivor of the wizard who tried to kill him. He is left only with a lightning-bolt scar on his forehead, curiously refined sensibilities and a host of mysterious powers to remind him that he's quite, yes, altogether different from his aunt, uncle and spoilt, pig-like cousin Dudley.

A mysterious letter, delivered by the friendly giant Hagrid, wrenches Harry from his dreary, Muggle-ridden existence: 'We are pleased to inform you that you have been accepted at Hogwart's School of Witchcraft and Wizardry'. Of course, Uncle Vernon yells most unpleasantly, 'I AM NOT PAYING FOR SOME CRACKPOT OLD FOOL TO TEACH HIM MAGIC TRICKS!' Soon enough, however, Harry finds himself at Hogwart's with his owl Hedwig ... and that's where the real adventure – humorous, haunting and suspenseful – begins.

'This magical, gripping, brilliant book – a future classic to be sure – will leave children clamouring for a sequel.' (Ages 8–13) – Karin Snelson

WORDS **TIM STREET**

GAME INFO

IN BRIEF Take the controls of a variety of Rebel ships, beat the Dark Side and stay alive in the greatest *Star Wars* moments ever.

DETAILS

PRICE	TBC
PUBLISHER	Activision
MULTIPLAYER	No
GBA LINK UP	No
BROADBAND	No

STAR WARS ROGUE LEADER: ROGUE SQUADRON II

Exclusive to GameCube, this sci-fi shoot 'em up is your only chance to fend off the Empire as leader of the Rebel Alliance's Rogue Squadron. If you loved the original trilogy this is the only *Star Wars* game to come close to recreating the films.

Imagine a game where you take control of the X-Wing through the Death Star Trench Run or where you take down the AT-ATs as they march across the icy plains of Hoth. Imagine if that game existed. Well imagine no more because this game is real and it's only on Nintendo GameCube from May 3.
Rogue Squadron II is every Star Wars fan's dream because it gives you the chance to take part in classic movie moments from the first three films; *Star Wars*, *The Empire Strikes Back* and *Return of the Jedi*. The game begins with an epic dogfight over the Death Star, culminating in the classic Trench Run at the end of the stage. Should

you complete the first mission you will even see the Death Star explosion that's been lifted straight from the film. How's about that for a first level!
Five different *Star Wars* craft are available to use – the X-Wing, Y-Wing, A-Wing, B-Wing and Snowspeeder and there are a host of awe-inspiring and detailed levels through which you can fly these vehicles. Real time lighting casts shadows off every craft and building, day turns to night as you race to complete certain missions and panoramas appear to stretch for miles, especially on Hoth's captivating ice wastelands. TIE Fighters screech across the sky, R2-D2 bleeps and burps and even the actor who

1. Can you match the skills of Luke Skywalker down in the Trench Run?

2. Take flight into the universe of *Star Wars* in loads of fab craft.

3. Down Walkers with the cable.

4. Avoid TIE fire and destroy the Death Star's gun turrets.

"*Rogue Squadron II* gives you the chance to take part in classic movie moments from the film trilogy."

played Wedge Antilles has been signed up to create a sensational audio experience. The game also takes advantage of Dolby Pro Logic, so if you've got a compatible TV the game's music and sound will make you feel as though you are sitting in a Rebel cockpit with the mother of all dogfights going on around you. The GameCube's controller's built in rumble pack also means that even slight grazes from enemy lasers will cause the controller to vibrate in your hands. *Rogue Squadron II* isn't simply a matter of blasting the hell out of the Empire either as an important strategic element has been included as part of the action. Part of your strategy will see you having to tell your wingmen whether to attack a particular installation, form up or flee the scene. Droid buddy R2-D2 is also on hand to repair your craft if your ship appears to be on its last legs. But make sure you

make it quick because the sheer pace and ferocity of the dogfights means that just one false move or an eye off the screen for a split second will result in certain death. The game also raises the gaming stakes thanks to the incredible intelligence of Darth Vader's forces. TIE Fighters will attack from all angles and just when you think you've got them on the run, they will evade your attacks and alter their course. You will also have to keep your finger close to the trigger because the better your performance, the more chance you will have of being awarded a medal. Perform competently and you'll open up the game's secrets and they include the chance to get behind the controls of the greatest *Star Wars* vessel of them all, the Millennium Falcon. This game certainly doesn't do things by halves. ■

VERDICT

A SYNCH TO GET THE HANG OF AND A SCI-FI TREAT TO PLAY AND HEAR, THIS IS LOOKING LIKE THE BEST *STAR WARS* GAME ON ANY HOME CONSOLE. THANKS TO THE RANGE AND DEPTH OF THE 11 MOVIE BASED MISSIONS, *STAR WARS* FANS HAVE NEVER HAD A GAME THAT COMES SO CLOSE TO RECREATING THE ORIGINAL *STAR WARS* TRILOGY UNTIL NOW.

From 'Nintendo Gamecube' leaflet produced by HMV in association with *Nintendo Official Magazine*

125

T Text level: reading

Exploring how reviews persuade

Questions 1–4 are about the review of *Harry Potter*.

1 Read the text closely.

a) How does this online review of a book differ from a book review in a magazine or a newspaper? Think about:

- who is likely to read the review

- how much time they will spend reading it

- what information they will need.

b) What evidence can you find in this text that the writer thinks the reader will not know anything about Harry Potter? Pick out quotations to support your answer.

2 Copy out the sentence below:

Then, in an absurd, magical twist of fate you find yourself surrounded by wizards, a caged snowy owl, a phoenix-feather wand and jellybeans that come in every flavour, including strawberry, curry, grass and sardine.

a) Underline all of the extended noun phrases you can find. (Remember – these are all the words that describe the noun.)

b) Write out the main sentence without any of the subordinate clauses. (Subordinate clauses are additional chunks of information within the sentence – take them out and the sentence still makes sense.)

c) Why do you think the writer uses subordinate clauses and expanded noun phrases in this sentence?

3 Read the quotation from Karin Snelson at the end of the review.

a) How can you tell that this was written before Harry Potter became famous? Quote from the text to support your answer.

b) Scan the *Star Wars* review to find the quotation given there. Why do reviewers often include quotations like this?

c) Compare Karin Snelson's quotation with that included in the *Star Wars* review. What differences do you notice and how do you account for these?

4 Imagine you have only read this review of this book and knew nothing else about Harry Potter. Would this review make you want to read the book? Why? What else would you want to know about the book before you bought it?

Questions 5–9 are about the *Star Wars – Rogue Leader: Rogue Squadron II* review.

5 Read the text closely.

a) What evidence can you find that this text is not only reviewing a product but also trying to sell it? Use quotations from the text to back up your answer.

b) Find and note down three examples of words or phrases that the writer uses to convey the excitement of the game being played.

6 This review is divided up into a main piece of text with a heading, several photographs and four smaller chunks of text. Read carefully each of the smaller chunks of text and suggest what the purpose of each chunk of text is.

7 Re-read the first section of the review from 'Exclusive to GameCube …' to '… Hoth's captivating ice wastelands.' How does the writer make it clear that he or she is writing for an audience familiar with the *Star Wars* films? Use quotations from the text to support your answer.

8 Read the section from 'TIE fighters … ' to '… certain death' on page 125. In this part of the review the writer uses several techniques to establish a close relationship with the reader. Find examples from the text of each of the following techniques listed:

a) writing as if talking to the reader, using the pronoun 'you'

b) writing as if imagining what will happen when the reader plays the game for him- or herself

c) writing as if on the side of the reader, heroically fighting a dangerous enemy.

9 Summarise in your own words three key strengths of the game which are identified by the writer.

 W Word level

Using dictionaries effectively

A dictionary can be a really useful resource not only for working out the meanings of difficult words, but also for giving the reader an insight into why the writer has chosen to use a particular word. Read the following dictionary definitions:

Example

epic (n) 1 a long poem narrating the deeds of one or more legendary or heroic figures; 2 a book or a film based on an epic narrative or hero [Gk. Epos 'song' or 'word']

classic (adj) 1 a) of the first class; of acknowledged excellence; b) remarkably typical; 2 a) of an ancient Greek and Latin literature, art or culture [based on Latin classis 'class']

1 What do the abbreviations 'n' and 'adj' mean?

2 Dictionaries often offer more than one definition of a word. Where there is more than one, how does the compiler of the dictionary decide which to put first?

3 What does the abbreviation 'Gk' mean?

4 Why is information about where words come from useful?

5 Use your own dictionary to look up the words 'epic' and 'classic'. What differences can you find between your dictionary definitions and the ones above? Explain why there may be these differences. Think about what readers the dictionary is designed for and what their needs might be.

6 Now read the following sentences from the *Star Wars* review.

Rogue Squadron II is every Star Wars fan's dream because it gives you the chance to take part in classic movie moments …

The game begins with an epic dogfight over the Death Star …

Using the dictionary definitions given, explain in your own words what the writer means when he or she describes movie moments as 'classic' and a dogfight as 'epic'.

Becoming a sub-editor

The job of a sub-editor is to tidy up and clarify an author's writing. Working with a partner, you are going to sub-edit the first two paragraphs of the *Star Wars* review from 'Imagine a game ...' to 'How's about that for a first level', which has arrived on your desk without any punctuation.

Imagine a game where you take control of the X-Wing through the Death Star Trench Run or where you take down the AT-ATs as they march across the icy planes of Hoth Imagine if that game existed Well imagine no more because this game is real and it's only on Nintendo Game Cube from May 3

Rogue Squadron II is every Star Wars fan's dream because because it gives you the chance to take part in classic movie moments from the first three films Star Wars The Empire Strikes Back *and* Return of the Jedi *The game begins with an epic dogfight over the Death Star culminating in the classic Trench Run at the end of the stage Should you complete the first mission you will even see the Death Star explosion that's been lifted straight from the film How's about that for the first level*

1 **a)** Your aim is to make the writing simple and easy to follow, while conveying a sense of the excitement of the game. Do not look at the original text on pages 124–125 as you work. You may use whatever punctuation you feel to be appropriate, but you must include:

- at least three exclamation marks
- a colon
- at least six commas
- two question marks.

b) When you have finished sub-editing the paragraphs, compare your punctuation with the original and decide which best meet the needs of the reader. Write a brief explanation of the similarities and differences and the effects they create.

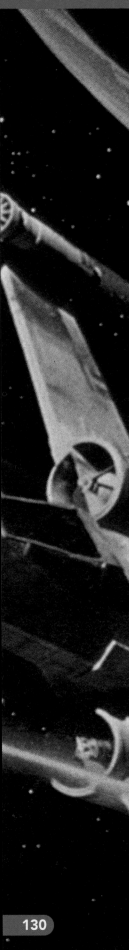

Head to head

When you want to present a case strongly in favour or strongly against something, you can present a **biased** argument. This means you try to create a version of the truth without telling any actual lies. There are two useful techniques you can use to do this:

- Use **ambiguity** – this means saying things that can have more than one meaning. Advertisers use ambiguity to avoid telling the exact truth.

Example

This computer game is the best I have ever played. This might mean that the game is very good or that the reviewer has only played one computer game ever.

- Leave information out – this is called **omission**. If part of the game you are reviewing doesn't work well – don't describe it. If the opening of the book is boring – don't mention it. If the CD is really expensive, avoid giving the actual price lots of advertisements simply say 'prices from…' to get round having to state the actual price. Similarly if you are trying to make the product seem worse than it is, then leave out all the good bits!

You are going to work in a pair. You have been asked to take part in a radio programme which recommends to its teenage audience new books, music, TV programmes and computer games that they might enjoy.

The format of the programme is that two people are invited: one to put forward an argument in favour of the programme, CD, book or game, and one to put forward an argument against it. They then discuss each others' reviews and try to prove that the other person's opinion is wrong.

Begin by agreeing with a partner what it is that you are going to review. Work together to list all the advantages and then all the drawbacks, then decide who will put forward the case in favour and who the case against. When you have done this, you should then work separately to prepare your arguments.

Writing to review

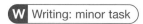 Writing: minor task

A review for a web page is presented quite differently from an ordinary review:

- The review needs to be short as readers tend to surf the net, moving quickly from one site to another.

- It needs to have an impact on the reader, so that he or she remembers it, so it is often highly visual, using animations and graphics.

- Images and icons that link to other websites and pages are often used to provide hyperlinks to further information.

Working with a partner, you are going to design a web page reviewing the *Star Wars* game *Rogue Leader: Rogue Squadron II*. Your aim should be to present a highly favourable review (approximately 150 words), likely to persuade the reader to buy the game.

With your partner you should:

- Re-read the review and discuss which information will persuade the reader to buy the game.

- Design your web page indicating the text you are going to include and any design features that your web page has.

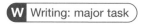 Writing: major task

You are now going to write a review of a new computer game in the style of the review of *Star Wars – Rogue Leader: Rogue Squadron II* on pages 124–125. The computer game could be one that you know about or you could invent your own. Your review is going to be included in a promotional leaflet that will be given out to customers in the shops selling the game. You should aim to write 300 words.

Think about what the key features of your game are:

- What type of game is it – action and adventure, sports or racing, arcade and platform, or a role-playing game?

- What is the main aim of the game? What obstacles and challenges do players face?

- How do the game's graphics and sound effects add to the gaming experience? Do you need any special accessories or equipment?

You may find the following writing frame helpful as you plan your work:

Headline giving the name of the product

First paragraph

- Include a short first paragraph that explains:
- what the product is
- why you should buy it
- what are its key strengths.

Exclusive to …

This is your only chance to …

If you loved the original, then …

Second paragraph

- Write a second paragraph which invites the reader to imagine playing the game.

Imagine a game …

Well, imagine no more …

How's about that …

Third and fourth paragraphs

- In the third and fourth paragraphs 'talk' the reader through playing the game.
- Highlight the key strengths of the game, but also alert the reader to the equipment he or she will need to play it.

The game has features such as …

To play the game you will need to have …

There are a host of detailed and awe-inspiring levels to work through, such as …

Part of your strategy will be to …

Make sure that …

Fifth paragraph

- In the fifth paragraph emphasise the challenge the game presents to the player.

This game raises the gaming stakes because …

Just as you think that …

You will have to …

Perform well and you will …

This game is …

Help box

1 Remember to indicate the images and captions that you would want to include in the leaflet to accompany your review.

Unit 12: Comment

When we speak we often offer our opinions to other people, but we rarely get a chance to develop them at length or in depth. Writing which **comments** on events or on issues gives the writer the chance to do just that. Usually organised chronologically, commentaries explore in depth issues of concern to the writer, coming to a conclusion based on their personal experience. You are now going to read two such texts, written by Kenyan and Jamaican writers. Both of them explore from very different perspectives what the idea of belonging to the British Commonwealth has meant to them in the past and what it means now. Before you read, find out as much information as you can about the British Commonwealth. Use an encyclopaedia, the library and the Internet to carry out your research.

'What does it mean to me? Nothing. Nothing. Nothing.'

Leone Ross
Jamaica

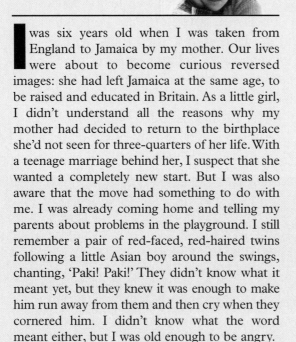

I was six years old when I was taken from England to Jamaica by my mother. Our lives were about to become curious reversed images: she had left Jamaica at the same age, to be raised and educated in Britain. As a little girl, I didn't understand all the reasons why my mother had decided to return to the birthplace she'd not seen for three-quarters of her life. With a teenage marriage behind her, I suspect that she wanted a completely new start. But I was also aware that the move had something to do with me. I was already coming home and telling my parents about problems in the playground. I still remember a pair of red-faced, red-haired twins following a little Asian boy around the swings, chanting, 'Paki! Paki!' They didn't know what it meant yet, but they knew it was enough to make him run away from them and then cry when they cornered him. I didn't know what the word meant either, but I was old enough to be angry.

Many years later Mum confirmed my suspicions, told me what she hoped Jamaican soil would do for me. She said she did not want me to be an 'ethnic minority' in Britain. 'Put her among black people,' she said. 'Then when she gets older she can go anywhere she wants.'

It was 1975 and the island was entering its adolescence: 13 years had passed since it had declared independence from British colonial rule and become part of the Commonwealth. At six years old, the Commonwealth meant nothing to me.

When I was asked to write this article, I rang up friends and family and did a quick vox pop: 'What did it mean to you to grow up in the Commonwealth?' There were lots of silences.

Then: 'The Commonwealth? You mean Jamaica/Australia/Barbados/Kenya/India/Canada?' The question seemed bizarre to all of us. I dug further: 'No, the Commonwealth. What does that mean to you?' The words flooded back: archaic, meaningless, colonialism, imperialism. And repeatedly: 'What does it mean to me? Nothing. Nothing. Nothing.' I suspect it means very little to a lot of English people as well.

I lived in Jamaica for 15 years of my life. Let me tell you about the circumstances in which the word 'Commonwealth' entered my brain. I cheered Jamaica at the Commonwealth Games. I was aware that our A-level results were sent back to England for marking, and that my stepfather, who is a solicitor, stood in front of black men in white wigs and made references to the British privy council.

Jamaica was a teenager when I got there, and like all teenagers, it was discovering its identity. Our national motto may be 'Out of many, one people', but we were still learning to value those of us who were dark-skinned after being devalued by a history in which our colonial government was as strangled by apartheid as South Africa. I know this because the nanny who was a second mother to me still wants to know if I have found a nice white man with blue eyes to have my own twins with. I know because black people all over the world spend a fortune on skin-bleaching and hair-straightening products.

So I can't tell you what growing up in the Commonwealth meant to me. But I can say what growing up in Jamaica meant to me. My mother was right. We all, whatever our origins, need somewhere to belong, where we are the majority. I belonged to a community and it's something I carry with me anywhere I go in the world.

© Leone Ross
From *The Guardian*

Dictionary check

colonial rule British government rule over its colonies
archaic old fashioned
imperialism belief in the right of a country to acquire colonies
apartheid policy of racial segregation
British privy council body of advisers chosen by the Queen

'Pleasethankyouwotnotpardon'

**Binyavanga
Wainaina
Kenya**

We sat, many years ago, watching Lady Di marry Charles. It would have been much better if the English royal family looked like I imagine colonial looters should look like: eagle-eyed, hooked noses, booming nasal voices. In Kenya, leaders were people you cowed to. It is hard to see a middle-aged lady with a perm and a handbag as the head of a colonialist empire that chewed up continents.

My late mother was several people to us: our intimate, our boss and an exotic person. Ugandan. My father is Kikuyu, a Kenyan. I remember sitting next to my mother, aged about 10, and she was shelling peas. I sat behind her, undoing her plaits with a comb, and she told me how sweet the Queen Mother looked, and how shy Diana was, and how surely Charles should find a way to pin back his ears.

During times like this, when the TV is on showing one thing for hours, one thing that didn't need one's complete attention (we were waiting for the vows and the kiss), other things come out in our languid conversations: how Kabaka Mutesa had found an official taster, and how you had to crawl to see him. How one sang 'God Save the Queen' at school. (Is she in trouble? I used to think.)

So this is the space the Commonwealth occupied in my mind. Where the files of royal pomp-laden things resided. We were probably the last generation of Kenyans who missed the colonial pomp – something we hate to admit. These days, people a year younger than me ask: 'Diana who? Didn't she do R&B or something?'

We cringed. Proud and ashamed at the same time, watching the Commonwealth Games and seeing some Kip-somebody win something long-distancy and have to present themselves to the Queen – or the Grand Duke of Commonwealth – they would surely laugh at his accent (we did), he would surely say something immensely stupid, something mannerless, something local. Did they say dinner? Would he cope with the forks and knives – pleasethankyouwotnotpardon. We laughed in school hearing the teacher say that Oginga and co appeared in London for the Lancaster House Conference wearing skins – ai! Skins!

Apart from Mugabe-mania, I haven't had reason to think of the Commonwealth for years. I was very jealous of how blasé the South Africans were when they were readmitted, when they considered *not* joining. Realising how little any of them cared, I wondered what the big deal was. We are now CNN people, Larry King people, MTV people – since Thatcher declared that foreign students pay fees, we run to America to seek cool, be seamless. 'This is London' is not our every morning as much as it was.

The Commonwealth always seemed part of everything larger then – but we have no real awareness of ourselves as part of the Commonwealth any more. We are finally starting to be Kenyan.

© Binyavanga Wainaina
From *The Guardian*

The opening ceremony of the 2002 Commonwealth Games

Dictionary check

looters robbers
cowed to were intimidated by
intimate close friend
languid slow-moving
Afrocentric focussed on an African viewpoint
Kabaka Mutesa former king of Uganda
Mugabe-mania the controversy caused when Zimbabwe, led by President Robert Mugabe, was suspended from the Commonwealth
blasé unimpressed

T Text level: reading

Exploring personal commentaries

Questions 1–4 are about the article 'What does it mean to me? Nothing. Nothing. Nothing.'

1 a) When Leone was a girl, what did she suspect were her mother's two reasons for wanting to go back to Jamaica? Refer closely to the text in your answer.

b) Explain in your own words what the writer means when she says that her and her mother's lives were about to become 'curious reversed images'.

c) What reason does Leone's mother give for returning to Jamaica? In what way did this confirm Leone's suspicions?

2 Look again at the third paragraph. Why is this paragraph so short? How does it link to the title of the text?

3 Leone offers two examples to back up her opinion that Jamaican people had not yet learned to value being dark-skinned.

a) In your own words, describe one of those examples.

b) What do you think the phrase 'like all teenagers, it was discovering its own identity' means?

4 Choose from the sentences below the one that best describes how Leone now feels about the Commonwealth.

a) It's an idea that does not have much meaning – her own community is more important to her.

b) She feels the Commonwealth is very important.

c) She hates the Commonwealth because of what it has done to the Jamaican people.

Question 5–7 are about the article 'Pleasethankyouwotnotpardon'.

5 Read the opening three paragraphs closely.

a) Explain in your own words the differences between how Binyavanga felt rulers should look and how the English royal family actually did look.

b) How do you think Binyavanga's mother felt about the English royal family?

c) What two pieces of evidence can you find to suggest that rulers in Kenya and in England behave very differently? Quote from the text to support your answers.

6 Make a list of the things that made Binyavanga 'proud' when watching the Commonwealth games and those that made him 'ashamed'.

7 Re-read the closing two paragraphs.

a) What surprised Binyavanga about South Africa's attitude to the Commonwealth?

b) Pick out two quotations from the text which show Binyavanga's attitude to the Commonwealth now.

8 How effectively do both writers give a personal commentary on the issue of the Commonwealth?

 W Word level

Uncovering layers of meaning

Your teachers will often ask you to 'read between the lines' by which they mean that they want you to go beyond what the words are saying and work out the meanings behind the words. Two useful technical words to describe this process are **inference** and **connotation**.

Inference is the process of using the information you have been given to make deductions and to draw your own conclusions.

Example

In the second article the writer describes:
How one sang 'God Save the Queen' at school. (Is she in trouble? I used to think.)
The reader can work out, without actually being told, that the writer was misunderstanding the words and the Queen was not actually in trouble. The reader can infer that the writer understands this and can make a joke of it. The reader has looked at the evidence given and come to a conclusion about it.

Connotation is the word we use to describe all the associations that a word builds up over time. In the first article the writer rings up her friends to ask them what the word 'Commonwealth' meant to them. Their answers are examples of what the word connotes – its associations.

Example

colonialism ——— Commonwealth ——— imperialism
meaningless ———   ——— archaic

1 a) Write down on a piece of paper the word 'adolescence', then write down all the words you associate with it in a spider diagram. These are the connotations that the word has for you.

   b) Re-read the third paragraph in the first article. Why does the writer describe Jamaica as entering its adolescence, and what is being inferred about colonial rule? (You may find it helpful to refer to the paragraph beginning 'Jamaica was a teenager …' to help you answer this question.)

S Sentence level

How punctuation is used for effect

1 Read the following sentence that is taken from the first article:
Our lives were about to become curious reversed images: she had left Jamaica at the same age, to be raised and educated in Britain.

   a) Identify the colon in the sentence.

   b) Explain in your own words how the ideas in the second part of the sentence, after the colon, link to the ideas in the first part of the sentence.

   c) Write your own sentence comparing your lifestyle with the lifestyle that your parents or carers had when they were your age, using exactly the same punctuation.

   d) Briefly explain why the writer used the colon in the sentence.

2 Read the following sentences, also taken from the first article: [Mum] said she did not want me to be an 'ethnic minority' in Britain. 'Put her among black people,' she said. 'Then when she gets older she can go anywhere she wants.'

a) Change what Leone's Mum said from direct to reported speech.

b) Why did the writer choose to use direct rather than reported speech for these words?

3 Re-read the third paragraph from the article 'Pleasethankyouwotnotpardon'.

a) Identify the two sentences in parentheses (brackets).

b) What do the two sentences have in common? What effect does the use of parentheses have on the reader here?

c) In what way is the content of these two sentences different from the content of the rest of the paragraph?

SL Speaking and listening

Radio show interviews

You are now going to comment on your own lifestyle and culture in a similar way to the writers you have been reading. You are going to work with a partner who has an interest in something you know very little about – it might be a particular form of music, fashion, politics, sports or interests, or they may belong to a different ethnic or religious group from your own.

You are going to prepare a radio show interview with this person, in which they are given the opportunity to explain all about their particular interest. In your pair you will need to take turns in being the interviewer and the person interviewed. Follow the instructions on the next page to help you to prepare the interview.

- Begin with a preliminary interview in which you ask your partner to talk to you generally about this aspect of their life. It's important that you show an interest in what they are saying, asking open questions such as 'What led you to become involved in your interest?', that enable them to provide you with interesting details. You will need to take notes as they talk.

- Then work with your partner to go through your notes and identify the most interesting aspects of what they have said for inclusion in the radio programme. Decide on the five questions you are going to ask them in the actual interview. You will need to prepare a brief introduction and conclusion to the interview.

You will then be ready to go 'live'. You can either perform your interview in front of the class or record it to be played back later.

Writing to comment

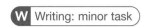

W Writing: minor task

A newspaper has included an article with the following headline: 'Teenagers: What are they good for?' and in it the writer criticises teenagers for the lifestyles they lead.

Write a 100-word letter replying to this article in which you write about a positive aspect of being a teenager in Britain today. You can choose to write about any aspect of teenage culture with which you are familiar. You could use the ideas from your Speaking and listening activity. You should offer a well-informed commentary – using evidence and examples to back up the points you are making – about the aspect of teenage life you have chosen to write about.

W Writing: major task

You are going to write a personal commentary on the community or communities to which you, as a teenager, now belong. You may choose to write about your own family and friends or other groups of people with whom you spend time. You can go back to the work you did for the Speaking and listening activity and use this as a basis for your commentary.

The title of the writing is 'Where I belong', but you should also choose a sub-title which relates to what you will be saying in your commentary.

You may find the writing frame below and on page 142 helpful as you plan your writing.

Where I belong

Opening section

Begin by describing the community to which you belong. Remember that a commentary has to offer not just a description but also personal opinions. Include examples of your community:

- using quotations from people who belong to it
- incidents that have happened
- details that bring it alive for your reader who may not know anything about it.

I belong to an unusual …

I have a group of friends who are for me, the most …

Other people might like hanging around in their spare time, but what I like best is …

Not many people know about …

The most important thing that happened to me was when I joined …

Second section

Use the second section of your essay to describe your personal experiences of living in this community, explaining clearly:

- how it has shaped your identity
- what you have learned from belonging to it
- what you like and dislike about it.

I've had many interesting experiences as a result of belonging …

It's with these people that I have my very best times, because …

I know more about myself because …

Belonging has made me …

Although there are aspects I don't like, what I really appreciate is …

Third section

- Explain what other viewpoints there are about your community – what those people who don't belong to it feel about it.

- Offer your own commentary on their views, making it clear what you feel about other people's opinions of your chosen lifestyle.

Of course not everybody sees it this way ...

The most difficult thing for people outside to understand is ...

I think that what other people say does matter, but ...

Fourth section

- Write about what you would miss if you were no longer part of the community.

- Try to think ahead and anticipate if you are likely to move away from it, and what this would mean to you.

I sometimes imagine what it would be like if ...

At the moment I feel that ...

In the future I may feel differently because ...

Final section

- Draw together the different parts of your essay in a brief concluding paragraph which summarises for your reader what you feel about the community or communities to which you belong.

I've tried to explain what I feel about ...

From this you can tell that ...

My community has made me ...

Review of revision objectives

R2 Synthesise information

An important skill that you will need for your key stage 3 tests is that of being able to select information from across a whole text (rather than from just one or two paragraphs) and then to organise that information into a clear answer to the question you were asked. Often these answers carry high marks – so it's useful to practise these kinds of questions.

Look back at the article 'Blow for teens' TV time' on page 113. Skim-read it to remind yourself of what it is about. Then look at the following question:

In the whole text, identify and comment on how the writer presents a balanced view of the research being described.

It's important to spot the key words in the question, so that you know exactly what you are setting out to do in your answer. The key words here are: 'identify', 'comment' and 'the whole text'.

Begin by identifying and noting down the words and phrases you can find that show the writer is presenting a balanced view of the research on TV and its links with violence.

Keep these notes very brief. Each note should cover:

▶ the point you are making

▶ a short quotation

▶ a brief explanation of the point.

Remember, you must draw your information from the whole article. The first two notes have been made for you.

> • **Point:** writer careful not to say that research definitely links violence to TV
>
>   **Evidence:** uses phrases such as 'more likely', 'might', 'may be'
>
>   **Explain the point:** choice of words shows researchers not yet certain about the link between violence and TV watching.
>
> • **Point:** writer says that some people do not believe this research
>
>   **Evidence:** 'unproven', 'flawed'
>
>   **Explain the point:** writer gives evidence from people who don't believe in the link as well as from people who do.

When you have completed your notes, select the four strongest points and write your response to the question. Remember to check that you have organised your answer in a clear and logical way, making sure you have drawn on information from the whole text.

In English there are three test papers:

- **The Reading paper**
- **The Writing paper**
- **The Shakespeare paper**

You should feel confident that the test papers will not ask you to do anything you have not covered in key stage 3. This section will help you focus on the key skills that you have developed.

The Reading paper

- This is **one hour and fifteen minutes** in length. In this time you are allowed fifteen minutes' reading time.

- You will be given a reading booklet, which will contain **three different texts**, and which will be linked by a theme, for example three texts about rescues. These texts will be chosen from a range of genres, including short stories, advertisements, diaries, newspaper reports, etc.

- You will also have a question booklet which will contain **approximately 15 questions** worth between 1 and 5 marks.

- Some of the questions will require you to complete a **table** or **tick box** or pick out details from the text; some questions will require you to write **short answers** in your own words, whilst others will require **longer, more detailed answers**.

- The questions on the Reading test will assess **five different focuses** (these focuses are numbered 2–6). You are now going to look at each of these assessment focuses in turn and explore how to use your reading skills to answer these questions effectively.

Focus 2: understand, describe, select or retrieve information, events or ideas from texts and use quotation and reference to text

What you have to do

▶ **find suitable, accurate information**

▶ **explain it clearly in your own words as far as possible**

▶ **give an example, a quotation or reference from the text.**

Unit 13: Key stage 3 tests

1 Look at Simon's account in Unit 1 (pages 8–9).

In the first paragraph, what three actions did Simon take to control Joe's fall?

> Each sentence contains a separate action which is a good example.

Tom's answer

Simon threw himself backwards into the snow. He braced or pushed his legs to hold himself against the rope's pressure. Then he began to let the rope slide slowly until it stopped. ✓ ③

(3 marks)

> Where Tom uses a word from the text, 'braced', he makes a good attempt to explain it with his own phrase 'or pushed'.

> Now try these questions. Look back to the arrowed bullet points on page 144 to remind yourself what you have to do.
>
> Question 2 is about Simon's account from Unit 1 (pages 8–9).
>
> Question 3 is about Joe's account from Unit 1 (pages 10–11).
>
> Question 4 is about the 'Mountain building' text from Unit 4 (pages 40–41).

2 In the first two paragraphs, what effect did the pressure of the rope have on Simon?

(1 mark)

3 From the third paragraph, give three details that tell you exactly where Joe is.

(3 marks)

4 Go to the last section entitled 'The Andes'. Here some facts are given which have certain consequences or things that follow as a result. Read the paragraph and complete the table.

Fact	Consequence or result
Continuing uplift and tectonic activity	
Uplift was rapid	

(2 marks)

Focus 3: deduce, infer or interpret information, events or ideas from texts

What you have to do

▶ read a little more into the information given in the text

▶ work out what is happening by looking at clues in the text

▶ 'read between the lines' for something that is there but not obviously stated and then put this in your own words.

5 Look at Joe's account from Unit 1 (pages 10–11). Read the paragraph beginning 'The whitest flashes …' to '… did nothing'.

How can you tell from this section that Joe is in a state of shock? Quote three details and give your explanation.

The first two explanations are good and merit one mark each.

Amanda's answer

Quotation	Explanation
I heard, but never felt, the air from my body	This tells me that one of his senses was alive but that his sense of feeling had gone ✓
As in dreams, time had slowed	This phrase makes it seem that Joe is not really in touch with reality ✓
Open eyes staring into blackness, thinking they were closed	Here Joe seems to be unsure whether he can see or not ②

The choice of quotation is good.

The last explanation is missing some extra interpretation, such as 'the confusion about what his eyes see and what his mind is telling him is caused by the complete darkness around him'.

(3 marks)

Now try these questions. Questions 6 and 7 are about Joe's account from Unit 1 (pages 10-11).

6 From what Joe says in the first two sections of the text, how can you tell that he is ready to give up? Give three points and support each one with a quotation.

(3 marks)

Hint ▶ ▶ ▶ ▷

▶ Link your quotation and point to the main idea in the question.

7 From the two paragraphs beginning 'My torch beam died …' to '… down to me', what can you deduce about Joe's state of mind?

(3 marks)

Focus 4: identify and comment on the structure and organisation of texts, including grammatical and presentational features at text level

What you have to do

▶ **explain how text is put together**

▶ **comment on how the text is laid out to make it easier to follow**

▶ **show how certain words, especially those that direct you, are used and give examples to support your points.**

8 Look at the *Daily Mirror* report on the World Cup Final from Unit 6 (pages 62–63).

What makes the first paragraph effective? Give two reasons.

Rachel's answer

• The first paragraph is in bold type. This makes it stand out at the head of the article, so more people would be drawn to reading this.

• The paragraph has three sentences which all begin with 'This time'. This builds up excitement and suggests something exciting is going to happen.

(2 marks)

You should now be used to how marks are awarded. What mark would you give Rachel for her response?

Now try the practice question on the next page. This is a longer question with bullet points and in the test there would be a whole page given for your response.

Question 9 is about the *Daily Mirror* report on the World Cup Final from Unit 6 (pages 62–63).

Unit 13: Key stage 3 tests

9 Describe in what ways the presentation of this newspaper article is effective.

You should look at:

- the arrangement of information and the text;
- the use of photographs;
- the headlines and captions;
- how language is used.

(5 marks)

> The last bullet point is probably the most difficult one, so here is a little help. It focuses on **language**. Try to include comments on the following features in your answer:
>
> - use of pronouns in the first paragraph
> - the use of a rhetorical question
> - the use of single sentence paragraphs
> - the way 'but' and 'yet' are used at the start of sentences.

Hint ▶ ▶ ▶ ▷

▶ Use the bullet points to structure your answer. You will then make sure you cover the important aspects of a good answer.

▶ For each of the bullet points select two or three ways in which an effect is created. Then write a short paragraph, using simple sentences, that explain your choices and their effect.

Focus 5: explain and comment on writers' uses of language, including grammatical and literary features at word and sentence level

What you have to do

▶ **select certain words that are important to the writer's purpose**

▶ **find associations in certain word choices**

▶ **identify and comment on the different parts of speech (nouns, verbs, adjectives, adverbs)**

▶ **explain the effects of similes, metaphors or any other literary features**

▶ **identify different patterns and types of sentence**

▶ **connect all these to the effects they create.**

10 Look at Simon's account from Unit 1 (pages 8–9).

In the paragraphs beginning 'It needed no pressure …' down to '… and after Joe' Simon uses several powerful words. Select three and comment on their effect

Effective choice of powerful vocabulary.

Comment links violence of the sound to how this is unusual when attached to the object of a rope.

Sunita's answer

Word or words	Effect
Rope exploded	Violent sound, unusual as ropes don't usually explode, danger

(3 marks)

Can you complete the remaining two parts of the question?

Now try these practice questions. Look back to the bullet points on page 148 to remind yourself what you have to do.

Questions 11–13 are about the review of *Harry Potter* from Unit 11 (page 123).

11 Comment on the purpose of the lists in the long second sentence, which begins 'Then, in an absurd, magical twist of fate …'

(1 mark)

12 Find four adjectives which describe the book *Harry Potter and the Philosopher's Stone*.

(4 marks)

13 In the final paragraph of the review, what is the effect of the verb 'clamouring'?

(2 marks)

> **Focus 6:** identify and comment on writers' purposes and viewpoints and the overall effect of the text on the reader
>
> **What you have to do**
> ▶ **identify the intention or purpose of the writer**
> ▶ **comment on the structure or organisation of the piece**
> ▶ **select certain words or sentences that have been chosen for particular effect**
> ▶ **give examples and quotations from the text to support your points**
> ▶ **detect implications in the ways the writer expresses his or her ideas.**

14 Look at Joe's account from Unit 1 (pages 10–11).

Look at Joe's own account of his fall in the section beginning 'Then, what I had waited for ...' down to '... and did nothing.' Comment on the way Joe reveals his thoughts and feelings.

You should look at:

- the purpose of this description;
- the choice of words and the pattern of sentences;
- the way in which you can detect what is going through Joe's mind;
- the text by using quotation and references to support your points.

Emma's answer

The description of the cutting of the rope, even though Joe had expected it, shows it has a sudden effect on him. The first section includes the word "fall" several times to emphasise the distance Joe was falling. When he says "I fell fast, faster than thought", the "f" sound (alliteration) speeds up the line. He doesn't seem to be able to think ("No thought") and he seems to be out of his own body for a moment ("From above I saw myself falling").

She picks out several important words and says what effect some of her quotations have.

She describes a number of Joe's thoughts and feelings, backing up what she says by close reference to the text.

This dream-like state is broken as he hits the snow. The "cold wetness" shocks him and then he realises what is happening. This is where the fear kicks in. He puts in one simple sentence – "I was frightened" and then expresses it more vividly with the exclamation "Ahhh....NO!!." The "Ah" is made longer with extra letters and "NO" is in capitals and has two exclamation marks. This makes the reader hear what must have happened. Joe falls so fast that his scream died above him. He's falling faster than sound.

The next paragraph mentions "flashes" four times and he adds the adjectives "bursting, electric", which suggests pain. As the flashes fade, he can still feel "the pulsing messages in his body". ④

(5 marks)

She is aware that sentence length is important and she covers this focus well.

The ending of her answer tails off a little. However, this is an effective answer, covering the full range of bullet points and developing valid points with effective quotations.

Now try this practice question.

Question 15 is about the texts 'Mountain building' and 'Freaky Peaks' from Unit 4 (pages 40–41 and 42–43).

15 Comment on the ways these two texts give information about the formation of mountains.

You should:

- comment on the structure of the texts;
- pay attention to the language and choice of words;
- use short examples and quotations to support your points;
- show awareness of the texts' intentions and the effects on the reader.

(5 marks)

Unit 13: Key stage 3 tests

The Writing paper

- This test is **45 minutes** in length.
- You will have an answer booklet to write in as well as **one page for planning** your ideas.
- There will be **one task** which will cover one of the four writing purpose 'triplets':
  - to **inform, explain and describe**
  - to **persuade, argue and advise**
  - to **imagine, explore and entertain**
  - to **analyse, review and comment.**

You will be assessed on the Writing paper for your ability to:

- write imaginative, interesting and thoughtful texts
- produce texts which are appropriate to task, reader and purpose
- organise and present whole texts effectively, sequencing and structuring information, ideas and events
- construct paragraphs, using cohesion within and between them
- vary sentences for clarity, purpose and effect
- write with technical accuracy of syntax and punctuation in phrases, clauses and sentences
- select appropriate and effective vocabulary
- use correct spelling.

You are now going to look at four practice tasks that each cover a different writing purpose triplet.

Focus: inform, explain, describe

What you have to do

▶ **write in a style that shows an awareness of audience**

▶ **write in a clear, factual manner, ordering your information and suggestions into clear sections**

▶ **use an appropriate choice of words to explain clearly what should be done**

▶ **use accurate spelling and punctuation.**

IMPROVE YOUR LOCAL PARK

A park in your area has become rather run-down and neglected. The people who use the park include parents with young children, teenagers and older people. The local council are due to hold a meeting to discuss how the park can be improved.

Write a report to the local council, outlining the problem and giving your ideas for improving the site.

Hint ▶ ▶ ▶ ▷

▶ Remember to use the planning page to jot down the ideas you have. A good plan will help you organise the structure of your response, as well as ensuring that your original ideas are not forgotten.

▶ You should also include in you plan reminders as to the techniques you will use in your response, such as bullet points.

Dominic has started his report with two headings. This shows a clear sense of purpose and focuses attention on the problem area.

Dominic's answer

To the Easton Council - Parks and Recreation Department

Re: Alexander Estate Play Area

The park that I am concerned about is the small play-area and gardens on the Alexander Estate, situated on the corner of Crawford Avenue and North Road.

He then goes on to give a clear, informative description of the location.

Sentence control is clear and accurate and present tense is used to outline the problem.

For a number of years it has been neglected and it is now in a very run-down state. There are several problems:

There is a variety of sentences and Dominic avoids overuse of 'There is ...' and 'There are ...', a common fault in this style of writing.

- The railings are broken in many places. Some of them are sharp and dangerous.

- The gate has been removed and not replaced. This means that young children can easily get out onto the busy North Road.

- The play equipment is broken, covered in flaking paint and quite dangerous. The slide steps are cracked and some are missing. The seats on many of the swings are broken.

- The garden area is overgrown and full of weeds. Litter, broken glass and rubbish has not been cleaned up for some time. The lawns become mud patches when it rains, and in dry weather they are like dust-bowls.

The next section gives a general point about the problem and he uses bullet points to describe and explain the exact problems.

- Many of the benches are damaged. You can't even sit on some of them.

As you will see from the details I have given, this is not a pleasant area. It is supposed to be for young people, but it has become more of a danger area than a play area. It will be just a matter of time before someone is injured. There is an urgent need for action.

I would like to suggest a number of ways in which this facility could be improved. It would not take a great deal of money to make the area better for the whole community – children and their parents and the old people, too, who use the park.

> The vocabulary used is appropriate. There is some awareness of audience shown in the use of formal language.

- First of all, replace the wooden fence with metal railings.
- Secondly, fix the gate with a secure fastening.
- Cover the play area with rubberised flooring, so that it is safe for children.
- Repair the broken seats on the swings and replace the missing steps on the slide.
- Arrange for a regular visit from the Cleansing Department, so that the litter doesn't build up.
- Put in some litter bins in the shape of cartoon animals for the younger children, the sort that don't easily topple over.
- You <u>could</u> ask one of the local people to look after the garden area.
- Change the benches. Concrete benches <u>would</u> be the best for long life.

> The suggestions section is controlled by using imperatives (instructions) to suggest actions to be taken.

> He uses 'could', 'should', and 'would' in appropriate and effective ways.

These suggestions could easily make our little park a much nicer and safer area for the whole community. We would be very grateful for your attention to our request.

Councillor Adam Johnson has been to look at the park and he agrees that something should be done. I hope that you will listen to my views, which represent the whole area. When Councillor Johnson presents this report with his own views I hope that the Council will be able to take action. This is what the Council should do for the community. The Council represents the people, so everyone hopes to see some action.

> Overall this response will score highly for its composition and effect, structure and organisation and sentence structure and punctuation.

> Dominic ends the report in an effective way by expressing a hope for action.

> Now try these practice tasks. Look at the bullet points underneath each focus to remind yourself what you have to do.

Focus: persuade, argue, advise

What you have to do

▶ **present a clear outline**

▶ **express your ideas (and those of others) in a fair manner**

▶ **argue your case with supporting evidence**

▶ **persuade others (i.e. the general public)**

▶ **organise your ideas in a clear developed manner**

▶ **use language that is appropriate and sentence structures that suit your purpose**

▶ **use accurate spelling and punctuation.**

Your school is organising a charity event to raise money for Children in Need. The headteacher, Mrs Smith, is trying to encourage as many people as possible to support and attend the event.

Write an article for your local newspaper to persuade the public to support your school's Charity Event in aid of Children in Need.

You should:

• outline the planned event;

• explain how the money will be raised;

• show how others will benefit;

• persuade people to take part by attending or contributing.

Focus: imagine, explore, entertain

What you have to do

▶ **write in a clear style that shows imagination**

▶ **show a clear sense of organisation and development in your writing**

▶ **add description to enable the reader to understand tour characters to create a sense of time and place**

▶ **engage the reader and make them want to read on**

▶ **use a lively choice of words and sentence patterns, possibly including some direct speech**

▶ **use accurate spelling and punctuation.**

This is an extract from a review of a *Star Wars* computer game.

'... where you take down the AT-ATs as they march across the icy plains of Hoth ... day turns to night as you race to complete certain missions'

You have been asked to write an imaginative story based on the ideas that are contained in the short extract.

- It could be about someone who becomes part of the computer game.
- You could set part of the story on the ice plains of Hoth.

Write your story.

Focus: analyse, review, comment

What you have to do

▶ **write in a style that analyses and expresses views about a situation in a clear, logical manner**

▶ **organise ideas in a clear way, making effective use of paragraphs**

▶ **use effective vocabulary in an interesting manner and vary sentence patterns to suit different purposes**

▶ **address the reader in an appropriate way**

▶ **use accurate spelling and punctuation.**

The Importance of Being Fit

It has been reported in the press that fewer young people are taking part in physical exercise. You have been asked to write an article for a young people's magazine about the benefits of sport and physical activities. You have been asked to cover the following points:

- The reasons why young people are not taking part in sports.
- The dangers that a lack of exercise brings.
- The benefits of taking part in activities.
- Ways of improving the situation.

Write the article for a young people's magazine analysing the issue of young people and exercise.

The Shakespeare paper

This paper is **one hour and fifteen minutes** long.

There are **two** sections with **one** question in each section.

In Section A, there is a **shorter writing task.** You should spend **30 minutes** on this section.

In Section B, there is a question testing your **reading and understanding** of the **two scenes** from the Shakespeare play you have studied. You should spend **45 minutes** on this section.

Section A: shorter writing task

The shorter writing task in this section will be linked to some of the themes and ideas from the Shakespeare play scenes that you have been studying, but does not require any reference to the play. It will cover one of the four writing purpose triplets, but **not** the same triplet that is covered on the Writing paper.

In this section marks will be awarded for:

- **sentence structure, paragraphing and punctuation** (6 marks)
- **composition and effect** (10 marks)
- **spelling** (4 marks).

Now try the practice task. Remember in the test you will have 30 minutes to complete this task.

Lady Macbeth tries to persuade Macbeth to go through with the original plan to kill Duncan.

Volunteers Required

Your Head of Year has asked you to write a notice that will be read by all Year 9 students, persuading them to take part in various ways in a Year 9 project. You should use one of the following ideas:

- the School Charity Appeal has asked each year group to organise its own sponsored event
- teams are required from Year 9 for different events in the Fun Day at the local park.

Write the text of your notice.

Unit 13: Key stage 3 tests

Section B: Shakespeare reading task

The question in this section will test your understanding of the two different scenes or parts of scenes from the Shakespeare play that you have studied. Extracts from the two sections will be included in the test paper and you should refer to these in your answer.

The question will assess one of the following focuses:

- **the motivation and behaviour of characters**
- **the way Shakespeare presents ideas**
- **the language of the text**
- **the text in performance.**

You should feel confident that your task will focus on one of these four ways of looking at the scenes. You may want to refer to other aspects in your answer. For example, it would be hard not to write about the way a character behaves and speaks if you were writing about directing the scene.

As you only have 45 minutes to answer the question in this section, you need to use your time sensibly. You should:

- Look closely at the key words in the question and ask yourself which assessment focus you are being asked to write about.

- Pay close attention to the extracts from the play included in the Shakespeare paper.

- Express your ideas clearly using carefully selected quotations and references from the extracts to support your points.

- Comment on how language is used. Pay attention to significant words (such as 'blood', 'darkness', etc.) and sentence structures.

- End your answer by referring back to the focus of the question.

- Avoid 're-telling the story' of the extracts. If you find yourself doing this, go back to the question and think about your ideas.

Unit 13: Key stage 3 tests

You are now going to look at four practice questions that each cover a different assessment focus. Using the guidance given, try to answer each one effectively. The practice questions are based on *Macbeth*, but you could easily adapt the style of question to scenes from *Twelfth Night* or *Henry V*, if you are studying one of these plays.

Focus: the motivation and behaviour of characters

What you have to do

▶ **make inferences about different aspects of Macbeth's character, his actions and what makes him behave in the way he does**

▶ **select appropriate references and close examples from both sections of the text to support your ideas**

▶ **comment on Shakespeare's use of language to present aspects of his character.**

1 Look at Act 1 Scene 7 from line 29 to end of scene and Act 5 Scene 3 (the whole scene).

What do we discover about the character of Macbeth in these two contrasting scenes?

Focus: the way Shakespeare presents ideas

What you have to do

▶ **select information and use quotation and reference to support your points**

▶ **identify and comment on Shakespeare's purposes and viewpoints**

▶ **comment on Shakespeare's use of language to explore the idea of deception.**

2 Look at Act 1 Scene 6 and Act 5 Scene 1, lines 30 to the end of the scene.

How does Shakespeare present the idea of deception in these scenes?

Unit 13: Key stage 3 tests

> **Focus:** the text on the performance
>
> **What you have to do**
>
> ▶ show understanding of what is going on in Macbeth's mind
>
> ▶ comment on his use of language using appropriate quotation and reference to the text to support your points
>
> ▶ explain his thoughts and feelings can be communicated to the audience.

3 Look at Act 1 Scene 7 lines 1–28 and Act 5 Scene 3 (the whole scene).

In these scenes, how would you want the actor playing Macbeth to show his thoughts and feelings to the audience?

> **Hint** ▶ ▶ ▶ ▶
>
> ▶ You need to focus on what is said (use quotations for key moments) and what is done (the key actions). You can then say how you would want the actor to respond. You can refer to the effect you would want from the audience.
>
> ▶ Try to keep to your own role in your answer – you are the director. You could refer to productions, workshops, videos that you have seen, but make sure that the short example you use supports your view.

> **Focus:** the language of the text
>
> **What you have to do**
>
> ▶ select information from the scenes and use quotations and examples to support your points
>
> ▶ comment in detail about Macbeth's use of language
>
> ▶ make inferences about his character from the different ways he speaks in the two sections.

4 Look at Act 1 Scene 7 and Act 5 scene 3.

In these extracts, how does Macbeth use language to reveal two sides to his character?